First World War
and Army of Occupation
War Diary
France, Belgium and Germany

50 DIVISION
151 Infantry Brigade
Royal Inniskilling Fusiliers
6th Battalion
1 June 1918 - 31 May 1919

WO95/2843/2

The Naval & Military Press Ltd
www.nmarchive.com
Published in association with The National Archives

Published by

The Naval & Military Press Ltd

Unit 10 Ridgewood Industrial Park,

Uckfield, East Sussex,

TN22 5QE England

Tel: +44 (0) 1825 749494

www.naval-military-press.com

www.nmarchive.com

This diary has been reprinted in facsimile from the original. Any imperfections are inevitably reproduced and the quality may fall short of modern type and cartographic standards.

Contents

Document type	Place/Title	Date From	Date To
Heading	WO95/2843/2 6 Bn, Royal Inniskilling Fusiliers 1918 June-1919 May.		
Heading	34th Division 103rd Infy Bde 6th Bn Roy. Innis Fus. Jun 1918.		
War Diary	Marseilles.	01/06/1918	03/06/1918
War Diary	In The Train.	04/06/1918	07/06/1918
War Diary	Le Pire	07/06/1918	17/06/1918
War Diary	Nandonne.	17/06/1918	17/06/1918
War Diary	Campagne.	18/06/1918	28/06/1918
War Diary	Desvres.	28/06/1918	28/06/1918
War Diary	Serqueux.	29/06/1918	30/06/1918
War Diary	50th Division 151st Infy Bde 6th Bn Roy. Innis Fusrs Jun 1918-May 1919 From Egypt 10 Div, 31 Bde.		
Heading	War Diary 6th Royal Inniskilling Fusiliers July 1918 Volume-XXXVII.		
War Diary	Abancourt.	01/07/1918	15/07/1918
War Diary	Martin Eglise.	16/07/1918	31/07/1918
Heading	War Diary 6th Royal Inniskilling Fusiliers August 1918 Volume-XXXVIII.		
War Diary	Martin Eglise.	01/08/1918	31/08/1918
Heading	War Diary 6th Royal Inniskilling Fusiliers September, 1918 Volume-XXXIX.		
War Diary	Martin Eglise.	01/09/1918	16/09/1918
War Diary	Sus-St Leger.	16/09/1918	26/09/1918
War Diary	Pierregot.	26/09/1918	28/09/1918
War Diary	Nurlu	29/09/1918	30/09/1918
Miscellaneous	Orders For Move. Appendix "A".		
Miscellaneous	Orders For Transport Move. Appendix "B".	27/09/1918	27/09/1918
Miscellaneous	Orders For Move. Appendix "C".	28/09/1918	28/09/1918
Heading	War Diary 6th Royal Inniskilling Fusiliers October 1918 Volume-XL.		
War Diary	Near Nurlu.	01/10/1918	03/10/1918
War Diary	Prospect Hill.	03/10/1918	03/10/1918
War Diary	Bony.	03/10/1918	03/10/1918
War Diary	Vendhuile.	04/10/1918	07/10/1918
War Diary	Le Catelet.	08/10/1918	08/10/1918
War Diary	Near Lecatelet.	08/10/1918	09/10/1918
War Diary	Maretz.	10/10/1918	16/10/1918
War Diary	Le Cateau.	17/10/1918	18/10/1918
War Diary	Le Trou Aux Soldats.	19/10/1918	29/10/1918
War Diary	Maurois.	29/10/1918	30/10/1918
War Diary	Le Cateau.	30/10/1918	31/10/1918
Miscellaneous	6th Royal Inniskilling Fusrs. Report on Operation of 3rd October 1918. Appendix "A".	03/10/1918	03/10/1918
Miscellaneous	Report on Operations of 17/18th October 1918. Appendix "B"	17/10/1918	17/10/1918
Heading	War Diary 6th Bn Royal Inniskilling Fusiliers November 1918 Volume-XLI.		
War Diary	Robersart.	01/11/1918	04/11/1918
War Diary	Foret De Marmal.	04/11/1918	04/11/1918

War Diary	Hachette.	05/11/1918	06/11/1918
War Diary	Noyelles.	07/11/1918	07/11/1918
War Diary	St Aubin.	07/11/1918	07/11/1918
War Diary	Dourlers.	07/11/1918	08/11/1918
War Diary	St. Remy.	09/11/1918	10/11/1918
War Diary	Monceau.	11/11/1918	30/11/1918
War Diary	Report on Operations 1st To 8th November 1918. Appendix "A".	01/11/1918	01/11/1918
Heading	War Diary 6th Royal Inniskilling Fusiliers 1st To 31st December 1918 Volume XLII.		
Miscellaneous			
War Diary	Monceau.	01/12/1918	05/12/1918
War Diary	Obies.	05/12/1918	31/12/1918
Heading	War Diary 6th Bn Royal Inniskilling Fusiliers January 1919 Vol XLIII.		
War Diary	Obies.	01/01/1919	31/01/1919
War Diary	War Diary 6th Royal Inniskilling Fusiliers 1st to 28th February 1919 Volume XLIV.		
War Diary	Obies.	01/02/1919	22/02/1919
War Diary	Englefontaine.	22/02/1919	28/02/1919
Heading	War Diary 6th Royal Inniskilling Fusiliers 1st to 31st March 1919 Volume XLV.		
War Diary	Englefontaine.	01/03/1919	28/03/1919
War Diary	Potelle.	28/03/1919	31/03/1919
Heading	War Diary 6th Royal Inniskilling Fusiliers 1st to 30th April 1919 Volume XLVI.		
War Diary	Potelle.	01/04/1919	30/04/1919
Heading	War Diary 6th Royal Inniskilling Fusiliers 1st to 31st May 1919 Volume XLVII.		
War Diary	Potelle.	01/05/1919	31/05/1919

wo 95 2843/2

6 Bn. Royal Inniskilling Fusiliers

1918 June - 1919 May

34TH DIVISION

ATTACHED 103RD INFY BDE

6TH BN ROY.INNIS FUS.

JUN 1918

2689

103
―――
34

Confidential

War Diary
of
6th Royal Inniskilling Fusiliers
from 1st to 30th June 1918

Volume XXXVI

June '18

Instructions regarding War Diaries and Intelligence Summaries are contained in F. S. Regs., Part II. and the Staff Manual respectively. Title pages will be prepared in manuscript.

WAR DIARY
or
~~INTELLIGENCE SUMMARY.~~
(*Erase heading not required.*)

Army Form C. 2118.

6th Royal [illegible]
Volume XXXV
June 1918 Page 1

Place	Date	Hour	Summary of Events and Information	Remarks and references to Appendices
MARSEILLES	1918 1st June		Arrived at MARSEILLES at about 6 a.m. Disembarked at about 1 p.m. & marched through MARSEILLES to No 5 Camp MUSSO. Disembarkation State – 30 officers 8[illegible] other ranks, of whom 3 officers ([illegible]) and 8 other ranks admitted to Hospital [illegible]	[illegible]
	2nd		Sunday – At MUSSO Camp	[illegible]
	3rd		Left Camp at 4.30 p.m.: arrived at [illegible] for entrainment at 8 p.m. train left at 10.15 p.m. Officers in carriages, men in closed trucks	
			24 men evacuated to Hospital today – [illegible] Officers, 21 Other Ranks & [illegible] joined Battalion at the train, having arrived at Marseilles on 29th May. Entraining state 36 Officers 871 Other Ranks	[illegible]
In the train	4th	11 am	Stopped at LE TEIL for a meal from 11 a.m. to 12 noon	[illegible]
		11 pm	Stopped again at PARAY-LE-MONIAL from 11 p.m. to midnight	
	5th	10 am	Stopped at MALESHERBES for a meal from 10 a.m. to 11 a.m. at JUVISY from 1 to 1.30 a.m. and at [illegible] from 9 to 10 p.m.	[illegible]
	6th	12 noon	Stopped at NOYELLES from 12 noon to 1 p.m.	[illegible]
		11 pm	Arrived at BERGUETTE at 11 p.m. and detrained	
LE PIRE	7th	1 am	Left BERGUETTE Station at 1 a.m. and marched to LE PIRE, near LILLERS. Battalion billeted in tents in 4 fields. Temporarily attached to 43rd Bde – 14th Division, together with 5th [illegible] & 2/4th [illegible] Infantry. 5 Other Ranks evacuated to Hospital today	[illegible]

A7092). Wt. W12839/M1293 750,000. 1/17. D. D & L., Ltd. Forms/C2118/14.

Instructions regarding War Diaries and Intelligence Summaries are contained in F. S. Regs., Part II. and the Staff Manual respectively. Title pages will be prepared in manuscript.

WAR DIARY
or
~~INTELLIGENCE SUMMARY~~.
(Erase heading not required.)

Army Form C. 2118.

6th Royal Inniskilling [illegible]
Volume XXXVI
[illegible] 1918 [illegible] 2

Place	Date	Hour	Summary of Events and Information	Remarks and references to Appendices
LE PIRE	1918 [illegible]		Kit, Rifle, S.A.A. inspections. Box Respirator drill. 4 men to Hospital today.	HCB
	9th		All Companies marched to LA LACQUE (about 7 miles away) this morning for baths, but no baths were available. 7 men to Hospital today.	HCB
	10th		All Box Respirators tested by Divl. Gas Officer today. 9 men to Hospital today.	HCB
	11th		Battalion inspected by G.O.C. X Corps this morning. 5 men to Hospital: 6 men rejoined from Hospital.	HCB
	12th		All companies working on 2nd line – at CANTRAINNE & BEAUREPAIRE. 3 men to Hospital today.	HCB
	13th		Work as yesterday. 6 Officers & 4 NCOs went up to view the front line – ST FLORIS, NE of ST VENANT. 1 man to Hospital.	HCB
	14th		Work as yesterday. 6 Officers & 4 NCOs went up to view front line. Lewis Guns firing on range. 2 men to hospital.	HCB
	15th		Work as yesterday. Lewis Guns firing on range. 8 men to Hospital. 3 men on leave to U.K.	HCB
	16th		Sunday. No work today – Battalion standing by ready to move. 9 men to Hospital today. 3 men on leave to U.K.	HCB
WANDONNE	17th		Battalion left LE PIRE at 9.30 a.m. and marched to WANDONNE a distance of about 20 miles, arriving about 6 p.m. About 90 men fell out on the way owing to attacks of malaria, 42 of whom were evacuated to Hospital. The remainder rejoined during the evening. Lorries with rations and blankets went astray & have not yet turned up.	HCB
CAMPAGNE	18th		Battalion left WANDONNE at 10.00 a.m. and marched to CAMPAGNE-LEZ-BOULONNAIS (a distance of about 10 miles) arriving	HCB

A7092). Wt. W12839/M1293 750,000. 1/17. D. D & L., Ltd. Forms/C2118/14.

Army Form C. 2118.

WAR DIARY
or
~~INTELLIGENCE SUMMARY.~~
(Erase heading not required.)

Instructions regarding War Diaries and Intelligence Summaries are contained in F. S. Regs., Part II. and the Staff Manual respectively. Title pages will be prepared in manuscript.

[illegible] Volume XXVI [illegible] [illegible]

Place	Date	Hour	Summary of Events and Information	Remarks and references to Appendices
CAMPAGNE	1918 [illegible] contd.		at 2 p.m. About 50 sick men brought on by lorry. 13 men [illegible] to Hospital. Battalion quartered in billets in the village. [illegible] attached to 103rd Bde. 34th ~~[illegible]~~ Div. Lorries with rations & blankets arrived at 10 p.m. [illegible]	
			Kit, Rifle & S.A.A. inspections. Arms Drill & Box Respirator Drill.	[illegible]
	19th		2 men to hospital today	
	20th		Battalion (excluding Transport) inspected [illegible] today by G.O.C. 34th Div. [illegible] 9 men to hospital today	[illegible]
	21st		Training today: 6.45–7.15 a.m. 9 a.m. to 12 noon and 2–3.30 p.m. Two companies working on the construction of [illegible] range & assault course at LE FAY. 9 men to hospital – 1 man rejoined from hospital.	[illegible]
	22nd		Work and training as yesterday. [illegible] to DESVRES today for disinfection & clean underclothing also drawn. [illegible] of men per day to the United Kingdom has been [illegible] to the Battalion commencing today. 11 men to hospital – 2 men rejoined from hospital. Several cases of [illegible] throughout the battalion – about 150 reporting sick daily.	[illegible]
	23rd		Sunday. 13 men to Hospital today – 1 man rejoined from hosp.	[illegible]
	24th		Work & training as on Saturday. 8 men to hospital 5 [illegible]	[illegible]
	25th		do. only 1 to hospital	[illegible]
	26th		do. 4244 Pte P. [illegible] died today ([illegible])	[illegible]
			30 men [illegible] to hospital.	

A7092). Wt. W12839/M1292 750,000. 1/17. D. D & L., Ltd. Forms/C2118/14.

Instructions regarding War Diaries and Intelligence Summaries are contained in F. S. Regs., Part II. and the Staff Manual respectively. Title pages will be prepared in manuscript.

WAR DIARY
or
~~INTELLIGENCE SUMMARY.~~
(*Erase heading not required.*)

Army Form C. 2118.

6th Royal Inniskilling Fusiliers [illegible]
Vol. [illegible]
June 1918 — Page 4

Place	Date	Hour	Summary of Events and Information	Remarks and references to Appendices
CAMPAGNE	1918 27th June		Training today as usual, but no work on range. Battalion standing by ready to move. Pte Quinn buried in CAMPAGNE Churchyard at 7.30 am. No to Hospital today – 1 rejoined from Hospital	[illegible]
	28th		Battalion left at 11am & marched to DESVRES where they entrained at 3pm. Marching out state 29 officers [illegible] – [illegible] other ranks. Over 100 sick conveyed to DESVRES by [illegible] 11 men evacuated to Hospital	
DESVRES				
SERQUEUX	29th		Arrived at SERQUEUX at 2.45 am, and detrained [illegible]. Marched to camp about 2 kilos NORTH of SERQUEUX where the Battn is under canvas. [illegible] reported sick today – no one to Hospital today.	
	30th		B Coy & Battalion Transport left at 5 pm today for new camp at ABANCOURT. 63 reported sick today – no one to Hospital. Casualties since the [illegible] of this war [illegible]:– 5 officers + 246 other ranks to Hospital [illegible] ([illegible] + 3.4/Rs [illegible]) 5 do [illegible] do [illegible] 46 do on leave to U.K. 6 do [illegible]	

A.H. Watson Lieut Col
Comdg 6 R. Innis Fus

30/6/18

A7092). Wt. W12839/M129? 750,000. 1/17. D. D & L., Ltd. Forms/C2118/14.

50TH DIVISION
151ST INFY BDE

6TH BN ROY. INNIS FUSRS

JUN ~~JLY~~ 1918 - MAY 1919

FROM EGYPT 10 DIV, 31 BDE

34

151/50

Vol 3

WAR DIARY.

6th Royal Inniskilling Fusiliers.

July 1918.

Volume – XXXVII

28J

Instructions regarding War Diaries and Intelligence Summaries are contained in F. S. Regs., Part II. and the Staff Manual respectively. Title pages will be prepared in manuscript.

WAR DIARY
or
~~INTELLIGENCE SUMMARY.~~
(Erase heading not required.)

Army Form C. 2118.

6th Royal Inniskilling Fus
Volume XXXVII
July 1918 page 1

Place	Date	Hour	Summary of Events and Information	Remarks and references to Appendices
ABANCOURT	1918 1st July		A.B & C companies left SERQUEUX at 9 am and marched to ABANCOURT, arriving at about 1.30 pm. Distance about 12 kilos. Sick men carried in 6 G.S. waggons. Draft of 18 other ranks arrived this afternoon.	HJB
	2nd		Working today on squaring up camp & digging shelters against bombs from hostile aeroplanes	HJB
	3rd		One company on road making - remainder working on camp	HJB
	4th		2 companies working on range - 2 companies on bomb shelters. Draft of 70 other ranks joined today	HJB
	5th		Battalion training.	HJB
	6th		do. Issue of quinine at rate of 15 grains per man a day started today	HJB
	7th		~~Battalion training~~ HJB Sunday - No training	HJB
	8th		Battalion training also about one company working parties	HJB
	9th		do.	HJB
	10th		do.	HJB
	11th		do.	HJB
	12th		do.	HJB
	13th		do.	HJB
	14th		Sunday - No training	HJB
	15th		Moved today to MARTIN-EGLISE. Transport left by road at 7 a.m. Remainder of Battalion marched to ABANCOURT station & entrained at 10 am., arriving at ~~AB~~ MARTIN EGLISE at 3.30 pm. Entraining state - 23 officers 630 other ranks	HJB

D. D. & L., London, E.C.
(A8004) Wt. W1771/M2-31 750,000 5/17 Sch. 52 Forms/C2118/14

Instructions regarding War Diaries and Intelligence Summaries are contained in F. S. Regs., Part II. and the Staff Manual respectively. Title pages will be prepared in manuscript.

WAR DIARY
or
INTELLIGENCE SUMMARY.
(Erase heading not required.)

Army Form C. 2118.

6th Royal Inniskilling Fus.
Volume XXXVII
July 1918 - page 2

Place	Date	Hour	Summary of Events and Information	Remarks and references to Appendices
MARTIN EGLISE	1918 16th July		Day spent in fixing up camp etc. Battalion is now in 50th Div. 151st Inf. Bde	HCB
	17th		Battalion training	HCB
	18th		do	HCB
	19th		do. 44 other ranks rejoined from Hospital in Egypt	HCB
	20th		do 10 platoons on working parties	HCB
	21st		Sunday. Brigade Parade for C. of E.	HCB
	22nd		Battalion training	HCB
	23rd		do. 10 platoons on working parties	HCB
	24th		do	HCB
	25th		do.	HCB
	26th		do.	HCB
	27th		do. 12 platoons on working parties	HCB
	28th		Sunday - No training or working parties. Leave to United Kingdom temporarily suspended, until 28 days quinine treatment is completed.	HCB
	29th		Battalion training - 2 companies on working parties - 30 yards musketry range completed and one company firing all day	HCB
	30th		Battalion training - 1 coy on range	HCB
	31st		1 coy. on range - 2 companies on working parties in the morning, + the other 2 companies in the afternoon 1 company on gas tests (under Div. Gas Officer) in the morning, + one company in the afternoon. Hostile air raid tonight at 11 pm. Ration strength 24 officers - 643 other ranks	HCB

H.M.C. Procter Major
Comdg. 6th R. Innis Fus

1 8/18

D. D. & L., London, E.C. (A8004) Wt. W1771/M2031 750,000 5/17 Sch. 52 Forms/C2118/14

WAR DIARY VR 4

6th Royal Inniskilling Fusiliers

August 1918

Volume — XXXVIII

29J

Instructions regarding War Diaries and Intelligence Summaries are contained in F. S. Regs., Part II. and the Staff Manual respectively. Title pages will be prepared in manuscript.

WAR DIARY
or
~~INTELLIGENCE SUMMARY.~~
(Erase heading not required.)

Army Form C. 2118.

6th Royal Inniskilling Fus
Volume XXXVIII
August 1918 – page 1

Place	Date	Hour	Summary of Events and Information	Remarks and references to Appendices
MARTIN EGLISE	1918 1st Aug		Battalion training – 3 companies providing working parties	KOB
	2nd		Raining nearly all day – very little training in consequence	KOB
			Ration strength of Battalion 22 officers 656 other ranks	
			On leave 8 do 61 do	
			Details 5 do 54 do	
			Effective strength 35 do 771 do	
	3rd		All companies providing working parties today – in 2 reliefs, as usual	KOB
			All coys firing on 30x Range in turn	KOB
	4th		Sunday. Church services for 4th anniversary of war	KOB
	5th		Battalion Tactical exercise this morning	KOB
	6th		Training as usual	KOB
	7th		do 2 companies providing working parties	KOB
	8th		do	KOB
	9th		do 102 men went on leave today	KOB
	10th		Divisional Tactical exercise this morning	KOB
	11th		Sunday	KOB
	12th		Battalion Tactical exercise this morning	KOB
	13th		Training as usual	KOB
	14th		do 3 companies providing working parties	KOB
	15th		do	KOB
	16th		Brigade Tactical exercise	KOB
	17th		All companies providing working parties	KOB
	18th		Sunday – Divisional horse show at DIEPPE	KOB
	19th		Training as usual	KOB

A7092). Wt. W12839/M1293 750,000. 1/17. D. D & L., Ltd. Forms/C2118/14.

Army Form C. 2118.

Instructions regarding War Diaries and Intelligence Summaries are contained in F. S. Regs., Part II. and the Staff Manual respectively. Title pages will be prepared in manuscript.

WAR DIARY
or
~~INTELLIGENCE SUMMARY.~~
(Erase heading not required.)

6th R. Inniskilling Fusiliers
Volume XXXVIII
August 1918 - page 2

Place	Date	Hour	Summary of Events and Information	Remarks and references to Appendices
MARTIN EGLISE	1918 20th Aug.		Training as usual	[initials]
	21st		All companies providing working parties	[initials]
	22nd		Battalion Route march	[initials]
	23rd		All companies providing working parties	[initials]
	24th		Training as usual	[initials]
	25th		Sunday	[initials]
	26th		Training as usual - all companies finding working parties	[initials]
	27th		do	[initials]
	28th		do	[initials]
	29th		do all companies finding working parties	[initials]
			Ration strength of Battalion 30 officers 478 other ranks	
			On leave in UK 3 " 305 "	
			Retails 6 " 51 "	
			Effective strength 39 " 834 "	
	30th		Training as usual - Brigade night assembly scheme	[initials]
	31st		do	

1 9/13

C G Barton Capt
Comndg 6th R. Innis Fus

D. D. & L., London, E.C.
(A8004) Wt. W1771/M2731 750,000 5/17 Sch. 52 Forms/C2118/14

VR 5 151/50

WAR DIARY

6th Royal Inniskilling Fusiliers

September, 1918.

Volume — XXXIX

30 J

Instructions regarding War Diaries and Intelligence Summaries are contained in F. S. Regs., Part II. and the Staff Manual respectively. Title pages will be prepared in manuscript.

WAR DIARY

~~or~~

~~INTELLIGENCE SUMMARY.~~

(Erase heading not required.)

6th Royal Inniskilling Fusiliers

Volume XXXIX

September 1918 - page 1.

Army Form C. 2118.

Place	Date	Hour	Summary of Events and Information	Remarks and references to Appendices
MARTIN EGLISE	1918 1st Sept.		Sunday - usual Church parades	HOB
	2nd		Battalion training - 2 parties of 72 men each for Brigade working parties.	HOB
	3rd		Battalion training - as usual	HOB
	4th		Divisional Route march - ANCOURT; BELLENGREVILLE; ENVERMEU; ST NICHOLAS + ARQUES - about 13 miles. Fighting order. Capt + Adj. H.O. Bolton thrown from horse + evacuated to Hospital. Lieut. R.A. Heard appointed acting adjutant	HOB
	5th		2 parties of 66 each, working. Training as usual - all companies on 30x range. 5 men rejoined from leave; 7 men from Hospital in Egypt. Ration strength 31 officers: 521 other ranks	HOB
	6th		50th Divisional Boxing Contests commenced today. - 24261 Pte. Doody beat Sgt. A. Brose, 1st K.O.Y.L.I. in middle weights. 23041 Pte. Burman (light weight) beaten by Cpl. Hale, 2nd R. Munster Fus.	HOB
	7th		Battalion Training as usual. 50th Divisional Sports commenced today. 47 other ranks rejoined today - 9 from Hospital: 34 from leave: 4 from Div. Signalling School. Ration strength 32 officers 568 other ranks	HOB
	8th		Sunday - Services as usual. Divisional Sports continued. Divisional Shooting pool today - 10093 Pte. Taylor, J bracketted 1st with two others. 10486 Pte. Graham, G. bracketted third with three others. 32 other ranks rejoined from leave.	HOB
	9th		Battalion training and finding working parties. Divisional sports continued. Boxing - 19959 L/Cpl O'Hanlon, J beaten in semi-final of welters, 24261 Pte. Doody beaten in semi-final of middle-weights. 27 other ranks rejoined from leave	HOB
	10th		Divisional Sports concluded today. 2/Lt. L. Briggs-Lawrance 4th in 440x race. Battn. team in Tug-of-War beat 1st KOYLI's and then were beaten in semi-final by 5th R. Irish Regmt	HOB

(A8004) Wt. W1771/M2 31 750,000 5/17 D. D. & L., London, E.C. Sch. 52 Forms/C2118/14

Instructions regarding War Diaries and Intelligence Summaries are contained in F. S. Regs., Part II. and the Staff Manual respectively. Title pages will be prepared in manuscript.

WAR DIARY

~~or~~

~~INTELLIGENCE SUMMARY.~~

(Erase heading not required.)

Army Form C. 2118.

6th Royal Inniskilling Fus

Volume XXXIX

September 1918 - page 2

Place	Date	Hour	Summary of Events and Information	Remarks and references to Appendices
MARTIN EGLISE	1918 11th Sept.		Battalion training - as usual. 22 O.R's rejoined from leave	HOB
			Divisional tactical exercise today. 22 do.	
	12th		Ration strength - 32 officers - 695 other ranks	HOB
			Training as usual. Draft of 33 Other Ranks joined	HOB
	13th 14th		Divisional inter-platoon shooting competition today ~~Draft of 33 Other Ranks joined~~ 33 O.Rs rejoined from leave	HOB
	15th		Sunday - services as usual. 2 Officers + 30 Other Ranks rejoined from leave. Capt + Adj. H.O. Bolton rejoined from Hospital	HOB
	16th		Battalion entrained at ARQUES-LA-BATAILLE at 5.40 am. Detrained at BOUQUEMAISON at 3pm. and marched to billets at SUS-ST-LEGER. 1 officer + 61 other ranks (medically unfit) left behind at MARTIN EGLISE.	HOB
SUS-ST LEGER			Marching out state - 34 officers - 776 other ranks. 15 other ranks rejoined at SUS-ST-LEGER from leave	
	17th		Battalion cleaning-up. Kit inspections; interior economy &c.	HOB
	18th		Battalion on field firing range + usual training	HOB
	19th		All Lewis guns fired on range - usual training. 16 new Lewis guns received today, making Battalion establishment of 36 guns	HOB
	20th		Training as usual	HOB
	21st		All companies on field firing range - Hot Baths for all coys	HOB
	22nd		Sunday. Training in the morning. R.C. Church parade, morning. Voluntary C. of E parade in the evening.	HOB
	23rd		Battalion training exercise in the morning	HOB
	24th		do. do. concluding with firing on field firing range.	HOB
	25th		Very wet ~~then~~ today. Battalion getting ready for move. Transport loaded this evening. Fighting order inspection by Brigadier at 2.30 pm.	HOB

D. D. & L., London, E.C. (A5004) Wt. W1771/M2031 750,000 5/17 Sch. 52 Forms/C2118/14

Instructions regarding War Diaries and Intelligence Summaries are contained in F. S. Regs., Part II. and the Staff Manual respectively. Title pages will be prepared in manuscript.

WAR DIARY ~~or~~ ~~INTELLIGENCE SUMMARY.~~

(Erase heading not required.)

6th Royal Inniskilling Fus.
Volume XXXIX
September 1918 - page 3

Army Form C. 2118.

Place	Date	Hour	Summary of Events and Information	Remarks and references to Appendices
SUS-ST LEGER PIERREGOT	1918 26th Sept		Transport left at 5.30 am: Battalion embussed at 9 am, left at 10 am, proceeding via LUCHEUX, GROUCHES, DOULLENS, BEAUVAL, and TALMAS to PIERREGOT, arriving at 2 pm. Marching-in state - 38 officers - 766 other ranks. Billets at PIERREGOT very poor	Appendix "A" HOB
	27th		Battalion standing-by all day, packed up ready to move. Transport left at 10 am this morning. Destination FRICOURT sub-area Route - BEAUCOURT - CONTAY - WARLOY - HENENCOURT - MILLENCOURT - ALBERT.	Appendix "B" HOB
	28th		Battalion left by bus at 1 pm - destination MOISLAINS. Battle surplus left at 2.30 pm & marched to BERTANGLES. Battle strength: - HQ. Lt. Col. H.F. WATSON, Lieut G. R. R. Baillie (a/Adjutant), Lieut J. Rothwell, M.C. and Capt A. Hipwell, RAMC. and 50 other ranks: A. Coy: 2/Lt Love (O/c): Buchanan, Turrell, Quaile (Liaison) and Whiteside and 125 other ranks: B. Coy: Capt Lyndon, M.C: 2/Lt Daish, Little, Briggs-Lawrance, ~~Wilson~~ and 118 other ranks: C. Coy: Capt R. J. Sutton (a/O.C.) 2/Lts Lewis, Reid, Furey and 121 other ranks: D Coy: Capt Smyth (O/c): Capt. Hook (Liaison) Lieut Kelly, 2/Lt Hicks, Martin and 119 other ranks. Total Battle strength - 22 officers 533 other ranks. Battle surplus: HQ. 4 officers, 59 other ranks: A. Coy 1 officer, 28 other ranks: B Coy 1 officer 27 other ranks: C. Coy 2 officers & 17 other ranks: D. Coy 23 other ranks: Total Battle surplus 8 officers and 154 other ranks. With transport: - Major Greville, Lieut Watson & Lieut Heard and 52 other ranks.	Appendix "C"
NURLU	29th		Battalion stands by in camp all day awaiting orders.	HB
	30th		Battalion still standing by.	HB

H F Watson Lt Col
6th Batt. R. Innis Fus

D. D. & L., London, E.C. (A8004) Wt. W1771/M2 31 750,000 5/17 Sch. 52 Forms/C2118/14

Appendix "A"

ORDERS FOR MOVE.

1. The Division (less Artillery) will be transferred from Third Army to Fourth Army, MONTIGNY Area on Sept. 26th, personnel moving by bus.

2. Battalion will assemble for embussing in column of route (A.B.C.D.HQ) at 8.45.a.m. head of column at Western entrance to SUS ST. LEGER -, on SUS ST. LEGER - IVERGNY Road.

3. Companies will each detail an embussing Officer, who will report to Capt. R.M. Flook (Brigade Embussing Officer) at 8.30.a.m. Troops will be formed up immediately off the road on N. side and will be told off in groups of 25, 5 groups of 25 per 80 yards of road space.

4. Transport will pass starting point at crossroads on GRAND BULLECOURT - LUCHEUX Road just W. of T in TUILIE. at 5.55 a.m. Route LUCHEUX - L'ESPERANCE - HALLOY - THIEVRES - MARIEUX - RAINCHEVAL - ROPEMPRE - MOLLIENS. Field Officer of 150th Infantry Brigade will be O/C. column:-6th R. Innis. Fus transport will be at head of column.

Column will halt for 1½ hours at 11.30.a.m. when the horses will be watered and fed.

5. Lewis Guns (less 4 A.A. Guns) with 20 magazine drums per gun, (in tin boxes) will be taken in busses. Also signalling equipment, as laid down in Brigade letter "Communications in the "Attack" dated 21/9/18.

6. Mobile Reserve of Ammunition and L.G. Magazines, Tools and Grenades, and Medical Stores will be carried on limbers. Cookers, Water carts and Bicycles will move with the Transport. 1 Cook per Company will accompany the Cookers.

7. Surplus stores, Officers kits and mess stores will be carried on the baggage wagons. All stores, baggage &c. to proceed with the Transport will be loaded this evening.

8. 1 lorry for Officers kits and mess stores, dixies &c. will report at Battalion H.Q. at 7 a.m. tomorrow. All stores to be ready for loading at that hour. 2 Q.M. storemen, 2 Mess waiters, and 1 H.Q. servant will accompany this lorry.

9. Blankets will be rolled and carried on top of the pack.

10. Capt. R.T. Sutton and 1 N.C.O. per Company will be detailed as an advance party. They will report at Brigade H.Q. at 7 a.m. to proceed by lorry to MONTIGNY CHATEAU, where they will report to the Staff Captain at 9 a.m. These N.C.O's will be in possession of details of numbers of Officers and other ranks in their companies to be billetted.

11. Billets to be left thoroughly clean, inspected by an Officer of each company and the usual certificates rendered before embussing.

12. Rations for 26th will be carried on the man.

H. Bolton
Capt. and Adjt.
6th R. INNISKILLING FUS.

Appendix "B"

ORDERS FOR TRANSPORT MOVE. 27/9/18.

Reference Amiens 1/100,000.

1. Transport (loaded the same as yesterday) will be at the cross-roads due N. of M in MOLLIENS-AUX-BOIS at 10 a.m., forming up on the PIERREGOT-RAINNEVILLE road facing S. 151st Brigade H.Q. Transport will be at head of column, followed by 6th R. Innis. Fus.

2. Destination FRICOURT sub-area. Route BEAUCOURT-CONTAY-WARLOY-HENENCOURT-MILLENCOURT-ALBERT. Bivouac on arrival.

3. 500 yards distance will be maintaied between units. 50 yards between every 12 vehicles.

4. Sufficient water to be carried in petrol tins on the limbers to water the animals.

5. Column will halt for 1½ hours at 1 p.m. for watering and feeding.

6. Major G.C.F.F.Greville will be in command of the whole column.

H. Bolton
Capt & Adjt.
6th R. Innis. Fus.

Appendix "C"

ORDERS FOR MOVE. 28/9/18.

Reference LENS & AMIENS 1/100,000 maps.

Battle Strength

1. 50th Division (less Artillery) will move from present area to IIICorps Area today (28th inst). Destination of Brigade Group MOISLAINS area.

2. Battalion will embuss at cross roads 1000x W. of MOILLIENS at 1.15 p.m. falling in in column of route, ready to march off at 12.50.p.m. Head of column at A.Coy's billet facing S. Order of march A. B. C. D. HQ.

Dress. Full marching order - change into Fighting Order in forward area. Kits should be adjusted so that this can be done as quickly and easily as possible.

3. Blankets will be carried on top of the pack. Balance of rations for 28th will be carried on the man.

4. Boxes for Lewis Gun magazines will NOT be taken into battle, but will be dumped with Battle Surplus Stores. Magazines will be carried in the web carriers.

5. Facilities are being made whereby Officers can take their valises, if they desire to do so. Such valises should be dumped at Guard room at once.

Valises to be left behind and surplus kits to be dumped with battle surplus at once.

6. Cooking utensils for Battle strength and Officers mess boxes will be dumped at the guard room by 12 noon, ready to be conveyed to the forward area by lorry. 2/Lt. D.Reid will be in charge of and travel with the lorry. He will be provided with AMIENS, & LENS maps 1/100,000.

7. Marching out States (in duplicate) showing Battle strength only, will be handed to Adjutant before marching off.

H Bolton
Capt & Adjt.
6th R. Innis. Fus.

ORDERS FOR MOVE. 28/9/18

Reference. 1/100,000 AMIENS maps.

Battle surplus

1. Battle surplus portion of Battalion will move to BERTANGLES, marching off at 2.30.p.m. Route - RAINNEVILLE - COISY. Dress - Marching order. Band and Drummers will carry their instruments. Kits of Band and Drummers will be handed in to Canteen Dump to be conveyed by lorry.

2. Blankets of Battle surplus will be rolled in bundles of 10 clearly labelled and dumped at the Canteen at once.

3. Officers Kits, Officers Mess stores ad cooking utensils for Battle surplus will be dumped at Canteen - Officers kits at once - Officers Mess stores and cooking utensils by 12.30.p.m.

4. R.Q.M.S. and Q.M. Storemen will be in charge of this dump and will proceed with the lorry conveying the baggage to BERTANGLES. A second journey will be made if all the stores cannot be conveyed in one lorry.

5. Lt-Col. H.MALLINSON, D.S.O. will be in command of all 50th Div. Battle surplus and other details. Major H.K. Crawford will be in command of 151st Inf. Bde. details.

6. Marching out states to be handed in before marching out.

7. Billets will be left thoroughly clean. C.Q.M.Sgts will be responsible for this. If possible certificate of cleanliness to be obtained from the Billet owners.

H Bolton
Capt & Adjt.
6th R. Innis. Fus.

151/50

WAR DIARY. Vol 10

6th Royal Inniskilling Fusiliers.

October, 1918.

Volume — XL.

31J

Instructions regarding War Diaries and Intelligence Summaries are contained in F. S. Regs., Part II. and the Staff Manual respectively. Title pages will be prepared in manuscript.

WAR DIARY or INTELLIGENCE SUMMARY.

(Erase heading not required.)

6th Royal Inniskilling Fus. Army Form C. 2118.

Volume XL -

October 1918 - page 1.

Place	Date	Hour	Summary of Events and Information	Remarks and references to Appendices
near NURLU	1918 1st Oct.		Battalion marched from BOOMERANG WOOD, near NURLU, to MALISSISE FARM, near EPEHY, and went into dug-outs there and at MAY COPSE	KOB
near EPEHY	2nd		Moved from MAY COPSE this evening to near BONY, to take up assembly positions for attack tomorrow morning	KOB
near BONY	3rd	0605	Battalion attacked at 0605 this morning and gained their objective (PROSPECT HILL near GOUY) (see report on operations attached)	Appendix "A"
PROSPECT HILL.			Major G. G. J. F. Greville assumed command of the Battalion for the operations.	
			Casualties: Officers 4 killed (Capt R.T. SUTTON, Lieut G.R.L. BAILLIE, 2/Lieuts C.A. HICKS and R.E.B. QUAILE). Wounded 7: (Capt. A.F.H. SMYTH, M.C., Lieut A.E. KELLY, 2/Lieuts M. MARTIN, H.C. LEWIS; D. REID; J. FUREY, H.A. WHITESIDE) 2/LT. F.J. LITTLE wounded and remained at duty.	
			Casualties: Other Ranks: 30 Killed: 186 Wounded: 19 Missing.	KOB
			Estimated number of Prisoners taken - 150 (receipts for 1 officer & 83 other ranks)	
BONY		2130	Battalion (less B. Coy & 2 platoons of D. Coy still attached to the Australians on the right) relieved by 7th Wilts Regmt at 9.30 pm. and returned to BONY	
VENDHUILE.	4th		Battalion marched to GILLEMONT FARM (A.13) - MONTBREHAIN 1/20,000 map) and later to trenches W. of KNOB WOOD - S.E. of VENDHUILE (A.19)	KOB
	5th		In trenches at KNOB WOOD. B. Company & 2 platoons of D. Coy rejoined this evening	KOB
	6th		Moved to TINO TRENCH and TINO SUPPORT - W. of VENDHUILE (X.30: F.6: A.1: MONTBREHAIN 1/20,000 map). Lt-Col. Watson left to command Battle surplus	KOB
	7th		Still in TINO TRENCH and TINO SUPPORT	KOB
LE CATELET	8th		Moved to VAUXHALL QUARRY - N.E. of LE CATELET (T.25)	KOB

D. D. & L., London, E.C. (A8004) Wt. W1771/M2-31 750,000 5/17 Sch. 52 Forms/C2118/14

Instructions regarding War Diaries and Intelligence Summaries are contained in F. S. Regs., Part II. and the Staff Manual respectively. Title pages will be prepared in manuscript.

WAR DIARY
or
~~INTELLIGENCE SUMMARY.~~
(Erase heading not required.)

Army Form C. 2118.

6th Royal Inniskilling Fusiliers
Volume XL
October 1918 - page 2

Place	Date	Hour	Summary of Events and Information	Remarks and references to Appendices
near LECATELET	1918 8th Oct.		Battalion bombed by hostile aeroplanes during night of 8th/9th 2 killed - 12 wounded.	HOB
	9th		Still at VAUXHALL QUARRY	HOB HOB
MARETZ	10th		Moved by 'bus to MARETZ - Transport rejoined Battalion at MARETZ Battle surplus left BERTANGLES, by train from POULANVILLE, at 4pm today	HOB
	11th		Battalion at MARETZ	HOB
	12th		Battle surplus rejoined Battalion at MARETZ Lt. Col. Watson remaining at ROISEL	HOB
	13th		Battalion reorganizing - training Lewis gunners etc.	HOB
	14th		do.	HOB
	15th		do. Lt-Col. Watson rejoined this evening.	HOB
	16th		Battalion left MARETZ at 2.30 pm. and marched to ESCAUFOURT ready to attack tomorrow morning. Transport, administrative details and Battle surplus marched to HONNECHY. Battle strength: Officers: HQ Major G. G. F. F. Greville, Lieut R.A. Heard (a/adj) Lieut H. St G Stewart, 2/Lt J Crawford, Capt A. Hipwell, RAMC: A Coy. Lieut G. L. Henderson, 2/Lt A. A. V. Buchanan: B. Coy Capt G. E. B. Lyndon, M.C., 2/Lts F. J. Little, J. N. Corscaden: C. Coy: Capt C. G. Barton, M.C. Lieut J. J. Kennedy. 2/Lt. V. J. F. Wilson D. Coy 2/Lts E. R. McKenney, G. Johnston: Liaison: 2/Lts B. A. Turrell, R. A. Rowe. Battle strength: Other Ranks: A Coy. 62: B. 84: C. 72: D. 78: HQ 41 - Total 337. Administrative Details + Battle surplus: Lieut-Col. H. F. Watson (at 50th Div. HQ) Major K. H. Crawford, Capts. E. N. Flook, H. O. Bolton (adj.)	HOB

D. D. & L., London, E.C. (A8004) Wt. W1771/M2 31 750,000 5/17 Sch. 52 Forms/C2118/14

Instructions regarding War Diaries and Intelligence Summaries are contained in F. S. Regs., Part II. and the Staff Manual respectively. Title pages will be prepared in manuscript.

WAR DIARY
or
INTELLIGENCE SUMMARY.
(Erase heading not required.)

6th Royal Inniskilling Fus — Army Form C. 2118.
Volume XL
October 1918 - page 3

Place	Date	Hour	Summary of Events and Information	Remarks and references to Appendices
MARETZ	1918 16th Oct.		Lieut G. S. W. Watson (Transport Officer): Lieut + Q.M. F. Turner: 2/Lt W. K. Baillie. Other Ranks: A 12: B 21: C 10: D 19: HQ 100 - Total 162.	HOB
LE CATEAU.	17th		Battalion attacked S. of LE CATEAU at 0520 in thick mist (see report on operations attached)	HOB Appendix B.
	18th		Attack continued and objectives gained. Battalion in support this evening.	
			Casualties: Capt C. G. Barton, M.C: 2/Lts J. N. Corcoran, V. J. F. Wilson killed on 17th: Lieut J. J. Kennedy wounded and died of wounds in C.C.S. 17th: 2/Lt C. R. McKenney, wounded + remained at duty 17th, killed 18th. Lieut H. St G. Stewart, 2/Lts J. Crawford, A. A. V. Buchanan wounded 17th.	
			Other Ranks: 17th Killed 11: Wounded 67: Missing 11 18th do 1 do. 5:	
			3 other ranks wounded 17th and evacuated to Hospital 20th (of the 11 missing - 9 were subsequently found to have been wounded and admitted to C.C.S).	
			Prisoners captured 17th + 18th - 9 officers - 246 other ranks - for which receipts were obtained.	
			War material captured 3rd 17th + 18th - about 54 machine guns; 8 anti-tank guns; 3 light trench mortars - 75 mm.	
LE TROU AUX SOLDATS	19th		Battalion marched to LE TROU AUX SOLDATS - arriving there about 4 pm. Battle surplus also rejoined at LE TROU AUX SOLDATS from HONNECHY	HOB
	20th		Battalion re-organizing - Divisional Church Parade in morning.	HOB

D. D. & L., London, E.C.
(A8004) Wt. W1771/M2731 750,000 5/17 Sch. 52 Forms/C2118/14

Army Form C. 2118.

WAR DIARY
or
~~INTELLIGENCE SUMMARY.~~
(*Erase heading not required.*)

6th Royal Inniskilling Fus
Volume XL
October 1918 - page 4

Instructions regarding War Diaries and Intelligence Summaries are contained in F. S. Regs., Part II. and the Staff Manual respectively. Title pages will be prepared in manuscript.

Place	Date	Hour	Summary of Events and Information	Remarks and references to Appendices
LE TROU AUX SOLDATS	1918 21st	Oct.	Battalion inspected by G.O.C. 151st Inf Bde at 9.30 am. Lieut-Col. H.F. WATSON, CMG, DSO left for duty with 50th Div. HQ. Major G.G.F.F. GREVILLE assumed command of the Battalion	KOB
	22nd		Battalion inspected by G.O.C. 50th Division at 12 noon. Rest of day spent in reorganizing + re-equipping also Lewis gun training	KOB
	23rd		Training – Tactical exercises, Lewis gun training etc.	KOB
	24th		do.	KOB
	25th		do.	KOB
	26th		do. Draft of 243 other ranks joined today, composed of South Lancs, Cheshires and Welsh Regiment (mostly Salonica Troops). Only 9 Inniskillings	KOB
	27th		Battalion training and reorganizing	KOB
	28th		do.	
	29th	11 am.	Battalion left LE TROU AUX SOLDATS at 11 am. and	KOB
MAUROIS		12.30 pm.	marched to MAUROIS, arriving at 12.30 pm	
	30th	2.30 pm.	Battalion left MAUROIS at 2.15 pm. and marched to	KOB
LE CATEAU		4 pm.	LE CATEAU, arriving at 4 pm	
	31st		Battalion left LE CATEAU at 2 pm and marched to ROBERSART and relieved 2nd R. Munster Fus. in front line. Relief completed at 6 pm. Battalion temporarily attached to 150th Bde	KOB

G.F. Greville Major
Comdg. 6th R. Innis Fus

D. D. & L., London, E.C.
(A8004) Wt. W1771/M2-31 750,000 5/17 Sch. 52 Forms/C2118/14

APPENDIX "A"

6th ROYAL INNISKILLING FUSRS.

REPORT on Operations of 3rd October 1918.

At Zero on the morning of 3rd October the 6th R. Inniskilling Fusiliers were in position as follows :-

B and D. Companies in position about 300x S.W. of Railway running through A.24.B. and A.18.C. A.17.B. The Boundary between Companies being a line drawn N.E. through C. in GRANDCOURT. B. Company was on the Right and D. Company on the left.

C.Coy. was in Support } in Sunken Road [illegible]
A.Coy. in Reserve }

The Orders for the attack were given verbally by A/Adjutant Lieut. [illegible] at about 0530 hours and were as follows :-

The Battalion will attack Prospect Hill.

D.Coy. on Left. B.Coy. on Right.

C.Coy. in Support to mop up Grandcourt and

A.Coy. in Reserve.

The Battalion was to follow close up to Barrage at Zero hour (0605 hours).

B.Company was to advance with left flank moving through C. in GRANDCOURT, its Right Boundary on Prospect Hill being roughly the line of wire running N [illegible].

At Zero hour the Battalion advanced in Artillery Formation of Sections in close co-operation with the Australians on the Right.

On reaching A.1[illegible].a.6[illegible]. B.Coy. with half D.Company, which had become detached, changed direction half left and advanced straight for PROSPECT HILL on a line straight under words PROSPECT HILL.

At 0800 hours the foot of Prospect Hill in B.1.D. was reached and a message was sent back to K.O.Y.L.I. in rear asking for support. A verbal message was received from Major de Houghton that he would send support.

B.Coy. pushed on to a line running roughly along contour 145 and proceeded to cut wire and mop up an enemy M.G. emplacement at B.2.Central at the request of the Australians. At this time this Company had 30 casualties in 5 minutes from Gun and M.G. fire from BELLEVUE FARM and from M.G. in B.7.A.5.5. The latter was seen to be mopped up later.

Another message was sent to K.O.Y.L.I. in the left Rear and to Northumberland Fusiliers who were the next troops in Rear at B.7.D.3.2. for assistance and the Company started to dig in on a line on contour 130.

No support reached the Company and the Australians did not get beyond B.2.B.1.6. so the position was consolidated with posts on this line and supports just south of Road.

This line was held for 2 days with the Australians and afterwards with 9th Devons with their left posts at B.[illegible].c.3.7.

There was a Platoon of Northumberland Fusiliers with which touch was obtained about B.1.c.9.8. No Australian troops were West of the WIRE at any time.

On arrival at A.18.Central touch between the two portions of D.Coy. was lost and the Support and Reserve Companies moved on a line between Road junction at A.18.[illegible] and A.12.c.5.[illegible], changing direction to the line of Woods running from A.12.c.5.2. to take in A.12.d.

A Machine Gun nest was located at Building at A.12.[illegible].2.4. which gave trouble. There was a deep canal in front of it. Orders were given for a platoon to move [illegible] of Lake taking advantage of cover given by the trees and work round the flank.

The nest was engaged and a Tank arriving on the scene bridged the canal at A.12.D.4.4. and parties were pushed over and the nest dealt with.

The advance was continued on to Prospect Hill, various M.Gs. being dealt with on the way. The Machine Guns on upper slopes of Prospect Hill did not put up a good fight.

"A"

The Battalion pushed forward over the crest of Prospect Hill and a hostile Battery was seen in action on Northern slopes. Fire was brought to bear on the Gunners, who retired in a N.E. direction over Prospect Hill and Battalion advanced to Guns, reaching Objective at 7.30 a.m.

Patrols were sent out to either flank to gain touch and as nothing could be seen of troops on either flank it was decided to consolidate and withdraw slightly from the advance position in which the Battalion was in.

Posts were put forward on N. slopes of the Hill with Supports under N. crest with a main line of resistance along line of upper road running through A.C.D. K.O.Y.L.I. were asked to send up one Company to fill up gap on our Right.

At 09.55 hours a message was sent to 151st Brigade giving dispositions, and informing them that one Company of K.O.Y.L.I. had been sent up to fill gap on our Right and were endeavouring to establish touch with troops on that flank.

At 10.22. a message was sent to O.C., K.O.Y.L.I. saying we were short of ammunition and asking if he could send any to us, and also inform Brigade.

At about 11.30 a Runner from B.Company arrived bearing a message from O.C., B.Company, he had been to Northumberland Fusrs. The message was as follows :-

"If you are our Brigade can you come here, am left with only 70 Rifles".

The Runner, when asked, could not say where B.Company was, as he had lost direction entirely, he thought he could find Northumberland Fusrs. A message was sent to O.C. Northumberland Fusrs asking him to send 2 platoons to support B.Company and that the Runner would act as guide.

At the same time a message was sent to O.C. B.Company by same Runner telling him of steps taken, asking him if he was in touch with Australians and directing him if possible to come to Battalion Headquarters, and telling him that Companies of K.O.Y.L.I. had filled the gap between us.

This message never reached O.C., B.Company.

At 12.25 a message was sent to Brigade asking for information regarding troops on our left as no touch could be obtained and reporting considerable trouble from both flanks from Machine Guns.

12.55 asking K.O.Y.L.I. for Liaison Runners.

No touch had up to this time been gained with K.R.R. and accordingly the line was extended to the Left as far as the S.E. outskirts of GOUY.

At 12 p.m. a message was received from O.C., D.Company, 2/Lt. Kelly, in which he stated that the enemy was counter-attacking on our left. Passed information to K.O.Y.L.I. and asked them to try and get in touch with K.R.R. and also to watch our left Flank. K.O.Y.L.I. replied that 4th K.R.R. had 2 Posts in front of village and that he could command its eastern approaches.

At 13.35 hours a message was sent to C.Company, K.O.Y.L.I. asking them to try and get in touch with our B.Company and support it.

At 13.27. O.C., K.O.Y.L.I. was informed by message that the situation of B.Company was obscure, last information received was that O.C., B.Company has requested support from Northumberland Fusiliers and K.O.Y.L.I. but that it was not forthcoming; asked him to try and locate. O.C., K.O.Y.L.I. replied that he had ordered Northumberland Fus. Company to send up 1 platoon to secure the Right of his C.Company in main Line of Resistance.

At 14.00 hours a message was received from Brigade Headquarters as follows :-

"Situation at GOUY not clear, enemy believed counter-attacking at moment AAA Hold out where you are if possible will support you. (Ends)"

At 14.28 hours Companies were ordered to push their posts further forward over the Ridge in order to gain better observation of ground and flanks. They were directed to send location of new positions.

A message was sent to Brigade at 14.45 hours asking for water, S.A.A. and S.O.S., also reporting trouble from Guns near

"A"

Goissancourt Farm.

Several Forward Posts withdrew from Northern slopes of the Hill, but were at once sent back. Enemy Machine Gun fire and Artillery Fire was very heavy at the time.

D.Company of K.O.Y.L.I. withdrew from Prospect Hill on account of this fire and casualties.

I at once ordered out 2 platoons from Main Line of Resistance to form a Defensive Flank and personally requested O.C., K.O.Y.L.I to send his Company back. A written message received from him at 15.15 hours to the following effect.

"Original position again taken up on top of Prospect Hill one Platoon Northumberland Fusiliers has reinforced my D.Company there"

At 5 p.m. D.Company report that posts now established forward at A.6.a.5.5. and A.6.b.3.3.

Touch not obtained with B.Company, Patrol still out.

A.Company one post at about B.1.B.0.5.

C.Company posts at about B.1.A.5.7.

Later the following message was received from K.O.Y.L.I.

"Following received from BUGO.

Following report from 7th Australian Infantry Brigade on your Right AAA 28th Battn is at present in trench System in B.2. as far as B.2.c.6.2. at least. I will at once endeavour to get in touch with your 2 Companies on Prospect Hill by pushing as far forward as trench junction at B.2.c.2.4.

There is no chance of counter attack on our front except from Reservoir which is being dealt with.

Later report states that Australians are now in touch with the platoon of Northumberland Fusrs. on our Right at B.1.D.70.50.

No mention of B.Company who were, according to later accounts from O.C Company, in touch with Australians.

At 6 p.m., O.C., D. reported that his patrol had returned but touch with B. had not been obtained.

At 6.25 p.m. O.C., D. reported that one of his Observers had seen the far Ridge lined with enemy and he was trying to verify same.

At 18.35 a message was sent to O.C.Coys directing them to push forward their advanced posts to vicinity of enemy trench running E and W. on N. slopes of Prospect Hill with supports under N. Crest of Hill, the Company on left paying special attention to ground to W. of Prospect Hill.

Extra Posts were now established at cross roads in GOUY by Reserve and Left Company was directed to get in touch with them. Companies were directed to be prepared to provide guides when called for as it was possible that the Battalion might be relieved tonight. Wounded and dead in front were to be collected and brought in after dark.

At 18.40 Brigade informed "All trace of B.Company has been lost. We have had patrols out trying to gain touch with them and K.R.R. Patrols have failed to find either. Water, S.A.A. not yet received. Posts have been established in Gouy, location given.

The Battalion was relieved by Wilts Regt. at about 9.30.p.m. and returned to ~~Gouy~~ [illegible]

GENERAL REMARKS.

The orders received by Battalion were that they should leave Gouy alone, as the K.R.R. would mop up that village.

Most of the casualties were suffered on Prospect Hill from enfilade fire from Machine Guns and Artillery. This fire continued during the whole of the day, practically without cessation.

The men behaved well under very trying circumstances.

The O.C., D. was wounded soon after starting.

O.C. C.Company was wounded also in the preliminary stages of the attack.

The A/Adjt, Lieut Baillie, was killed during consolidation on Prospect Hill

"A"

2/Lt. Reid was wounded twice on Prospect Hill but remained on duty with his platoon until relieved at night.

2/Lt. Lewis was also wounded on Prospect Hill and was evacuated.

2/Lt. Quaile was acting as Liaison Officer between the Battalion and 7th Y.R.R. and was killed in village of Gouy.

CASUALTIES.

Officers killed.
" wounded.

Other Ranks killed [illegible]
" wounded. [illegible]
missing [illegible]

G. H. Granville Major.

APPENDIX B

REPORT
on Operations of 17/18th October 1918.

The Battalion, under the command of Major G.G.F.F.Greville, paraded at MARETZ at 14.30 hours on the 16th October, and marched to the vicinity of ESCAUFOURT, where a halt was made for about six hours.

One Officer, and one N.C.O. from each Company, were sent forward at once to reconnoitre the route to the assembly position which was in the vicinity of the cross-roads at Q.27.B.45.25.

Brigade Operation Order No. 183, Copy I, dated the 16th, had been received at about 14.30 hours just as the Battalion was moving off. Battalion Operation Orders were issued to Companies at 20.45 hours, and a Conference of Company Commanders was held at Battalion H.Q. when final detailed instructions were issued to them.

Orders had been received that Battalion H.Q. must be established at the cross-roads Q.27.B.45.25 by 23.59 hours, Accordingly the Battalion paraded at 23.00 hours and marched via route Q.31 a & b - Q.32.a. - Q.26.c & d. and Q.27.d. a & b. The Battalion was there formed up about 50 yards in rear of the cross-roads in the order of battle, i.e. "C" Company, under Capt. C.G.Barton.M.C. on the Left, "A" Company, under Lieut. G.L. Henderson, on the Right, "D" Company 50 yards in rear of centre, under 2/Lieut. E.R. McKenney, "B" Company 50 yards in rear of "D" Company, in Reserve, under Capt. G.E.B.Lyndon. M.C. Battalion H.Q. were established about cross-roads Q.27.b.45.25.

The Battalion, on arrival, was met by a R.E. Officer, and the question of bridging the river SELLE was discussed. It was considered impracticable to put a bridge across before ZERO hour.

Amendment No.1. to Brigade Operation Order No.183, was received at 01.12 hours, giving fresh orders regarding the DOTTED RED LINE, which would now run as follows :- Q.23.d.9.9. - Q.17.Central - Q.10.b.9.2. - Q.4.c.5.2. SUGAR FACTORY exclusive.

The objective for the Battalion would now run from the BRICK WORK exclusive in Q.10.D. to the SUGAR FACTORY exclusive in Q.4.c.

Notification was received that at 04.00 hours a Post of 1 N.C.O. and 1 man of the Northumberland Hussars, would be stationed at the cross-roads Q.27.b.45.25. and reports "In Position" would be sent there for transmission to Brigade Headquarters.

Amendment No. 2. to Operation Orders No.183, was also received at 01.12 hours, which stated that two Trench Mortars would advance with the Battalion, each with 30 rounds. Four Trench Mortars would be placed in position on road about Q.28.c.2.4. during the night 16/17th inst. At Zero these guns would open a rapid rate of fire on the Railway astride point Q.28.c.8.5. which would be maintained until ZERO + 18 minutes.

Notification Order was received giving 05.20 hours as Zero hour. At about 02.00 hours the jumping off positions for the Companies were reconnoitred.

At 03.30 hours Companies were moved to a position further forward on to a line of hedges running above the road on about the 120 contour.

The R.E., assisted by the Pioneer Battalion, moved the bridges down into the road in vicinity of broken Bridge.

Touch had been gained early with 1st K.O.Y.L.I.

At 04.00 hours, Front line Companies were set in motion to gain Jumping Off positions WEST of ST. SOUPLET - ST.BENIN ROAD.

The Support and Reserve Companies moved into garden in front by slightly N.W. of Road junction with the broken bridge at Q.28.c.25.80.

The Trench Mortars were also moved to this position.

The Bridging area was as given on the attached diagram.

A Machine Gun had been located in the vicinity of a house at Q.28.c.30.80. which searched the road incessantly.

At Zero hour the Barrage opened and at the same time bridges were thrown across the river. The Officer i/c Trench Mortars was badly wounded and several of his men. The hostile Barrage was not long in opening. Some casualties were caused from short bursts of our guns.

Although the bridging was not a great success, chiefly due to the fact that the bridges were too short, the Battalion was got across and organized for the advance astride the Railway facing North, by Zero + 30 minutes. The Trench Mortars were not seen after the crossing of the river, due entirely to the fact that the Officer and a number of the teams were out of action.

At 05.50 hours, a message was sent to Brigade reporting the Battalion across the river.

At ZERO + 36 minutes the Battalion advanced astride the Railway, Much opposition being encountered. The Scottish Horse were now in close support behind Battalion Headquarters which advanced close behind the Support Company, with the Reserve Coy. The advance was continued as far as FASSIAUX Bridge, where strenuous opposition was encountered. The Reserve Company was now ordered to mop up houses in Q.28.a., which was done by one Platoon and prisoners taken. It was found necessary to further reinforce the front line in the vicinity of FASSIAUX Bridge, before the opposition was overcome and the advance continued.

At 07.30 hours a message was sent to the Scottish Horse asking for a Company to reinforce the Right from the Railway inclusive.

The next serious opposition encountered was in Q.16.Central from enemy in organized shell holes, but this was overcome after about ten minutes sharp fighting. The enemy at this point came out to meet us but many were shot down and the remainder retired. Two Sections were now sent from the Reserve Company to reinforce the Left, who had encountered opposition at the houses E. of Ford at Q.15.D.9.4. Shortly after this, the remainder of the Reserve Company and some elements of Scottish Horse, joined the Firing line. Serious opposition was encountered at the Railway junction Q.11.A., where we were held up for 30 minutes before the opposition was overcome. Many prisoners were taken at this point.

At 08.00 a message was received from Capt. Lyndon stating that he had reached S. end of detraining point and asking for reinforcements on his Left.

At 08.10 hours, Scottish Horse sent one Company to reinforce.

At 08.15 hours a message was sent to Brigade, telling them that we had reached S. end of Detraining Point and that the Scottish Horse were supporting us.

The position on the Right of the Railway was obscure owing to heavy mist.

At 09.01 hours, another message was sent to Brigade stating that we were still held up at S. end of Detraining Point, and asking for S.A.A., Bombs, as the Pack Mules, which had been sent for, had not arrived; also stating that we were trying to push ahead by utilizing 149th Brigade Stokes.

At 09.15 hours a message was received from the Right Company, (Lieut. Henderson) showing dispositions on MAP TRACE and stating that the Company was held up by Machine Gun fire from BRICK WORK, SLAG HEAP, PETROLEUM REFINERY and MALTINGS. He estimated his strength at 15 Rifles and gave his position on Railway platform about Q.10.Central.

At 09.40 hours another message was sent to Regtl. Dump telling the R.S.M. that S.A.A. and Bombs were urgently required and to send them up at once.

At 10.10 hours, another message was despatched to Brigade, asking for S.A.A. and Bombs and stating that we were still held up and requesting Tanks. At 10.30 hours a message was received from Capt. Lyndon, to say that the enemy were bombing their way into the Station buildings at S. end of Detraining Point. He also requested Bombs and S.A.A. and asked for a Barrage or Tanks.

At about 11.15 hours, an Artillery Officer came up and he was asked to give Artillery Support.

At about 11.30 hours, Pack Mules arrived with S.A.A. and L.G. Magazines, which were distributed amongst the Companies. At 11.50

hours, a message was sent to Capt. Lyndon telling him that Artillery Support had been requested and that S.A.A. and Lewis Gun Magazines had been sent up.

At 12.00 hours, Capt Lyndon reported that the enemy were again Bombing through the buildings.

At about 12.30 hours, the enemy was seen advancing in very extended order on the Railway from the line of the BRISK WORK and SLAG HEAP. These proved to be Light Machine Gunners, but they were met by a burst of fire from the Railway and the majority retired.

At 12.45 hours, a message was sent to Brigade, reporting this and again asking for Bombs to clear the buildings in the vicinity of the Detraining Point.

At 13.15 hours, a Situation Report was received from Capt. Lyndon in which he stated that he was now holding the buildings in the vicinity of Q.10.c.5.5. and the trench in rear and to the Left of the buildings. "A" and "D" Companies were unable to hold the advanced positions right of the Railway and had to withdraw as we were unable to support them. They now held the line of the Railway from Q.16.A.5.6. to Q.10.A.5.3. One Platoon of "C" Company held a position near the building at Q.10.c.5.8. while the Scottish Horse occupied the Trench near Q.10.c.5.8. and Northwards to about Q.10.A.3.0., also Trenches facing N.N.W. from Q.10.C.2.4. to Q.9.D.9.5. One Company of the Dublin Fusiliers occupied the SUNKEN ROAD from about Q.16.A.3.4. to Q.16.A.3.5. Battalion Headquarters were established at Q.16.A.2.6.

At 14.00 hours Scottish Horse attacked the PETROLEUM REFINERY and SLAG HEAP. "B" Company extended to their Left and occupied the Sector vacated. One Platoon of "B" Company mopped up for the Scottish Horse, although their Reserve Company was not used. The hostile Machine Guns on the Station still gave considerable trouble. "A" and "D" Companies now moved to the trenches near S. end of Detraining Point. "A" Company sent forward a party to mop up the buildings on the Detraining Point and established a Post at about Q.10.A.8.1. to cover the ground between the Scottish Horse on the SLAG HEAP and the Scottish Horse in the PETROLEUM REFINERY. All houses in rear were cleared by a party from "B" Company under 2/Lt. Crawford. A message from Lieut. Henderson stated that Scottish Horse were held up in the vicinity of the Buildings just S. of the Station. Touch was gained with one Company of Lancashire Fusiliers at the Chapel Bridge Mills. Owing to the admixture of Units and the doubtful position of the DOTTED RED LINE, Battalions were ordered to be grouped as follows :-

Scottish Horse }
Inniskilling Fusiliers } under Lieut.Col. Blair.
Northumberland Fusiliers }

The Battalion thus came under the orders of the 149th Brigade. A telephonic message was received by O.C., Group ordering the attack to be continued under a barrage at 17.30 hours.

It was now about 17.00 hours, and it was not considered possible to carry out the order owing to Units being so mixed. The order was consequently cancelled.

At 20.00 hours, the Scottish Horse requested reinforcements of twenty men and 2 Lewis Guns on the SLAG HEAP. These were sent at once under 2/Lieut. Corscaden who was killed almost immediately on starting. 2/Lt. Crawford was then detailed to command the party and succeeded in reaching the SLAG HEAP. A message was sent to O.C., "A" Company ordering him to establish a Post between the SLAG HEAP and the Left Post of the Scottish Horse who were in the Trench West of the Detraining Point. Orders were now received that Lt.Col. Blair's group would attack the Triangle at 21.00 hours under a creeping Barrage which would come down 300x in front of the line between the BRICKWORK and SUGAR FACTORY. Junction was to be made with 66th Division who were now on the Railway at Q.35.c.7.4. The attack was made by the Northumberland Fusiliers but did not gain the objective (Railway Triangle).

At 00.30 hours, a Warning Order was received which stated that if the 2nd Northumberland Fusiliers captured the Triangle, the Scottish Horse would capture the Wood in Q.5.c & d. and the line of the FINAL Objective, i.e. Red Line between Q.5.d.6.5. and Q.6.b.6.6. 2nd Northumberland Fusiliers would advance from the TRIANGLE to RED LINE between Q.6.b.6.6. and K.36.d.5.8. feeling their way along the Railway to Q.5.c.6.9 and K.36.d.5.8. keeping touch with 66th Division. The 6th Royal Inniskilling Fusiliers would support the Scottish Horse.

In the event of the TRIANGLE not being captured by the 2nd Northumberland Fusiliers, Scottish Horse would capture the TRIANGLE and advance to the RED LINE. The 6th Royal Inniskilling Fusiliers would capture the Wood in Q.5.c & d. and take the RED LINE from Q.6.d.6.5. to Q.6.b.6.6. The 2nd Northumberland Fusrs would support both Battalions.

At 03.45 hours, further orders were received which stated that the Barrage Line would be K.35.c.7.1. to Q.5.d.5.6 - Q.11.a.2.8. - Q.11.d.0.0.

The 6th Royal Inniskilling Fusiliers were now detailed to form up on the Right of the Scottish Horse, and to advance under the Barrage, mopping up the BRICKWORK and capturing the woods in Q.5.c & d. The Scottish Horse on our left were ordered to form up and to advance so as to establish the line along the east face of the Triangle and to form a defensive flank along the Railway to Q.6.a.0.1. 2nd Northumberland Fusiliers were ordered to prolong this line to Q.6.d.6.5 Zero hour was given as 06.30 hours. The Battalion formed up at 05.15 hours facing N.E. with its left flank resting on the road at Q.10.c.8.5. and at Zero hour advanced under a Barrage to the 1st Objective (BRICKWORKS). Battalion Headquarters had been moved to Trench about Q.10.c.4.5. at 05.00 hours.

At Zero the enemy put down an intense barrage along the East edge of the Railway and on the Detraining Point.

The BRICKWORK was cleared without casualties and the advance continued on the woods in Q.5.c and d and Q.11.a & b. The Wood was assaulted by one Company from the Western Edge and one Company from the South.

It was captured at 06.00 hours with the loss of only 1 Officer, 2/Lt. McKenney, and 1 Other Rank. Over 40 prisoners were taken in the Wood, along with three Trench Mortars and three Anti-Tank Rifles.

The position was consolidated and the 25th Division passed through. The Battalion was now placed in Reserve to the Scottish Horse and 2nd Northumberland Fusiliers who were holding the line of the Railway about the TRIANGLE facing North. Several casualties were sustained from Machine Gun fire during the day.

At 12.00 hours on the 19th, the Battalion was relieved and marched back to LE TROU AUZ SOLDATS. During the two days operations the Battalion captured 9 Officers and 238 Other Ranks. not counting many wounded who were evacuated through the Casualty Clearing Stations.

Our casualties were :-

	Officers.	Other Ranks.
Killed.	4.	14
Died of Wounds.	1	1
Wounded.	3	74
Missing.	-	1
Total.	8.	90

N O T E S.

The Tanks detailed to co-operate with the Battalion were unable to give any assistance owing to the heavy mist and smoke barrage. They would have been invaluable. The Battalion on our Right appears to have lost direction and moved too far to their Right, thus leaving a big gap.

This was one of the chief causes why the Battalion failed to reach its final objective. The BRICKWORK, as before stated, was not taken by the Battalion on our Right, and consequently it was impossible to advance further than Q.10.Central with the Battalion so reduced in numbers.

There was much Machine Gun fire from the BRICKWORK throughout the day.

It was not apparent from the maps given us, that the Station and Detraining Point contained so many buildings.

To clear these buildings properly and gain the final objective, which was from the SUGAR FACTORY to the BRICKWORK (exclusive) was a task too great for a Battalion of our strength. The frontage allotted to the Battalion being nearly 1000 yards.

The Tanks gave no support or help in any way.

W.K. Baillie 2nd Lt. for
MAJOR.

151/50

WAR DIARY

Vol 11

1st Bn Royal Inniskilling Fusiliers

November 1918.

Volume — XLI.

32J

WAR DIARY
or
~~INTELLIGENCE SUMMARY.~~
(*Erase heading not required.*)

Instructions regarding War Diaries and Intelligence Summaries are contained in F. S. Regs., Part II. and the Staff Manual respectively. Title pages will be prepared in manuscript.

Army Form C. 2118.

6th Royal Inniskilling Fus.
Volume XLI
November 1918 - page 1

Place	Date	Hour	Summary of Events and Information	Remarks and references to Appendices
ROBERSART	1918 1st Nov		Persistent hostile M.G. and artillery fire during night 31st/1st, both on front line and also support Companies and Battalion H.Q. Patrol (consisting of 2/Lt. R. A. Rowe, 1 N.C.O. & 4 men) encountered strong enemy post during night 31st/1st. 2/Lt Rowe, 1 N.C.O. & 1 man wounded and ~~mission~~ missing. 3 men rejoined - 1 unwounded & 2 wounded.	HOB
			Perfectly quiet during the day - no hostile firing and practically no enemy movement observed	
	2nd		Usual heavy artillery & M.G. fire from dusk to daylight - perfectly quiet during daytime	HOB
	3rd		Very much quieter during night 2nd/3rd and abnormally quiet during day	HOB
	4th	0745	D. Coy. left to proceed at Railway at DRILL GROUND corner.	
		0830	B & C. Coy attached farm buildings on ENGLEFONTAINE-LANDRECIES	
		0840	road, and established position astride the road by 0840.	
FORET DE MORMAL		1030	Battalion (less D. Coy) proceed to DRILL GROUND corner, arriving	
		1215.	there by 12.15. D. Coy. rejoined at DRILL GROUND corner	
		1230	Advanced through FORET DE MORMAL, astride ROUTE DE LANDRECIES.	HOB
		1630	Position consolidated from spur in B 20. D. to CENSE TOURY (Ref map. 57A. 1/40,000)	
			For narrative of operations of 1st to 8th November see Appendix "A" attached	Appendix "A"
	5th	0640	THE HALT captured	
HACHETTE		0840	HACHETTE captured & mopped up & line established along CANAL from B 29. C. 2. 9 to CULOT NOIRE thence through WOOD to about B. 23. D. 1. 7	HOB

D. D. & L., London, E.C.
(A8004) Wt. W1771/M2'31 750,000 5/17 Sch. 52 Forms/C2118/14

Instructions regarding War Diaries and Intelligence Summaries are contained in F. S. Regs., Part II. and the Staff Manual respectively. Title pages will be prepared in manuscript.

WAR DIARY or ~~INTELLIGENCE SUMMARY.~~

(Erase heading not required.)

6th Royal Inniskilling Fus. Volume XLI November 1918 - page 2

Army Form C. 2118.

Place	Date	Hour	Summary of Events and Information	Remarks and references to Appendices
	1918			
HACHETTE.	6th Nov.	0900	~~Bn~~ Battalion concentrated in WOOD N. of HACHETTE (B. 22. c.)	KJB
		1130	Moved to HACHETTE FARM (B 27. A)	
		1330	Left HACHETTE FARM and marched to billets at NOYELLES	
NOYELLES	7th	0600	Brigade left NOYELLES and marched to jumping off point at ST REMY CHAUSSEE (D 13. C 5. 1)	
		0815	Advanced from jumping off point, to 1st objective on ST AUBIN-AVESNES Road. After severe opposition, 1st objective gained	
ST AUBIN		11.15.	and consolidated by 11.15.	KJB
		1345	Advance continued to final objective MAUBEUGE-AVESNES Road. Very considerable opposition encountered and	
		1600	advance held up. Line consolidated for the night in sunken road D.18.D and along ST AUBIN-MONT DOURLERS	
DOURLERS.			Road, from D.18. D 7.7 to E. 13. c. 0. 8.	
	8th	0730	Advance to final objective resumed at 07.30 and final	
		0805	objective captured by 0805	
			Very considerable hostile artillery + M.G fire all morning. Enemy counter-attacked from 1100 to 1400, but failed to reach our advanced posts at any point.	KJB
		1530.	149th Bde (3rd Royal Fus.) passed through front line to continue the advance	
		1600.	Battalion marched back to billets at ST REMY CHAUSSEE (For full narrative of operations see Appendix "A")	Appendix "A"

D. D. & L., London, E.C. (A8004) Wt. W1771/M2 31 750,000 5/17 Sch. 52 Forms/C2118/14

Instructions regarding War Diaries and Intelligence Summaries are contained in F. S. Regs., Part II. and the Staff Manual respectively. Title pages will be prepared in manuscript.

WAR DIARY
or
~~INTELLIGENCE SUMMARY.~~
(*Erase heading not required.*)

Army Form C. 2118.

6th Royal Inniskilling Fus.
Volume XLI
November 1918 - page 3

Place	Date	Hour	Summary of Events and Information	Remarks and references to Appendices
ST. REMY	1918 9th Nov.		Battle surplus rejoined ~~Strength of~~ Fighting strength of Battalion after operations - 6 officers 275 other ranks. Ration strength; including Battle surplus and Administrative details:- 12 officers - 425 other ranks.	HJB
	10th	14.30	Battalion moved to MONCEAU	HJB
MONCEAU	11th		Battalion cleaning up and reorganizing Armistice signed	HJB
	12th		do. reorganizing and training	HJB
	13th		do do.	HJB
	14th		~~Divisional~~ Brigade memorial service to officers, N.CO's + men fallen in recent operations. Presentation of Medal ribands by G.O.C. 50th Division	HJB
	15th		Battalion training; cleaning up billets etc. Draft of 48 other ranks joined	HJB
	16th		do.	HJB
	17th		Sunday. usual services	HJB
	18th		Battalion training, improving billets &c. Schoolroom opened and classes started in French, Shorthand, Reading + Writing, Bookkeeping + Commercial Arithmetic	HJB
	19th		Training, Educational classes, Football, Sports &c.	HJB
	20th		do	HJB
	21st		do	HJB
	22nd		do	HJB
	23rd		do	HJB

D. D. & L., London, E.C. (A8004) Wt. W1771/M2-31 750,000 5/17 Sch. 52 Forms/C2118/14

Instructions regarding War Diaries and Intelligence Summaries are contained in F. S. Regs., Part II. and the Staff Manual respectively. Title pages will be prepared in manuscript.

WAR DIARY
or
~~INTELLIGENCE SUMMARY.~~
(Erase heading not required.)

Army Form C. 2118.

6th Royal Inniskilling Fus
Volume XLI
November 1918 - Page 4

Place	Date	Hour	Summary of Events and Information	Remarks and references to Appendices
MONCEAU	1918 24th Nov.		Sunday - usual services.	HOB
	25th	"	Inspection of billets &c. by G.O.C. 50th Division, usual training, educational classes, football &c.	HOB
	26th	"	do	HOB
	27th	"	do.	HOB
	28th	"	do.	HOB
	29th	"	do. Marching-order inspection by G.O.C. 151st Inf Bde	HOB
	30th	"	do.	
			21 officers posted to Battalion and joined for duty between 14th and 30th Nov. With 2 exceptions these officers are just commissioned and entirely without experience as officers. Ration strength today. 31 officers - 468 other ranks.	HOB
			Geo P Lyndon Major. Comndg 6th R. Innis Fus	
			30/11/18	

D. D. & L., London, E.C. (A8004) Wt. W1771/M231 750,000 5/17 Sch. 52 Forms/C2118/14

Inf. Maps
57A.N.W. 1/20,000

Appendix
'A"

REPORT ON OPERATIONS

[illegible] to 4th November 1918.

The Battalion, under command of Major [illegible] Greville, left LE CATEAU at 2 a.m. on 31st October 1918, marching to ROBERSART where they relieved the 2nd Munster Fus. in the front line being temporarily attached to 150th Infantry Brigade. Dispositions :- B. Coy. (under command of Captain [illegible] M.C.) on right from G.4.2.[illegible] to A.26.c.1.6. C. Coy. (under command of Capt. [illegible] Henderson) on left from A.26.c.1.5. to A.26.a.1.7. D. Coy. (under command of Capt. [illegible]) in support and A. Coy. (under command of Major W.G. Crawford) in reserve. Battalion H.Q. at A.26.b.3.0.
11th Bn. Royal Fus. (18th Division) on the left; 5th Northumberland Fus. on the right.
Battalion strength in the line :

HQ.	3 Officers		[illegible] Other Ranks	
A. Coy.	2	"	110	"
B "	2	"	102	"
C "	2	"	110	"
D "	2	"	103	"
Total	11	"	[illegible]	"

The Battalion remained in the line until the morning of the 4th November. During this period there was considerable hostile shelling and machine gun fire from dusk to daybreak, but, except for occasional sniping, the front was perfectly quiet during the daytime.

Patrols were sent out every night by both companies in the line to gain information as to the enemy's position and to endeavour to obtain identifications. On the night of 31/1st, 2/Lt. R.A. Love with 1 N.C.O. and 4 men encountered strong Machine Gun post at about A.26.a.[illegible]. 2 wounded and 1 unwounded men returned; 2/Lt. Love, 1 N.C.O. and 1 man were wounded and failed to return.

Total casualties 31st October to 3rd November :-
1 Officer, wounded and missing.
2 Other ranks killed.
11 " wounded.
2 " " and missing.

At 1800 hours on the 3rd November, Battalion came again under the command of 151st Infantry Brigade. Orders received for the operations of the 4th were as follows (Brigade Instructions Nos. 1 & 2 - Series B; Bde O.O.188 & 189 & B.M.326) :- Battalion (less 1 Company) to be in Brigade Reserve and to stand fast at ZERO hour (0615). At 0745, 1 Company to move to the Railway in G.10.a. and come under the orders of 4th [illegible]. At 0815 Battalion (less 1 Company) to capture and mop up FARM BUILDINGS (A.26.c.9.4.) establishing line astride this point on LANDRECIES - ENGLEFONTAINE Road. On completion of this operation Battalion to re-organise and move to DRILL GROUND CORNER (G.10.a) and await further orders there.

At 0750 D. Company left and proceeded across country to DRILL GROUND corner, coming under heavy shell fire almost immediately upon starting. Near ROBERSART enemy mine exploded causing heavy casualties (1 Officer wounded, [illegible] Other ranks killed, 26 wounded, 1 missing). They received no orders at DRILL GROUND Corner and waited there and rejoined Battalion on arrival.

At 08.30 B.Company on right and C. Coy. on left attacked LANDRECIES - ENGLEFONTAINE Road, converging inwards on to FARM BUILDINGS (A.26.c.9.4.) on reaching the road. Objective was gained at 08.50; heavy Machine Gun fire was encountered, but casualties were slight owing to the rapidity of the attack. Position was consolidated as ordered. Lieut. [illegible] Heard was wounded but remained at duty until the following day.

At 10.1[illegible] verbal message was received over the telephone from G.O.C. [illegible] Infantry Brigade, to move the Battalion down the LANDRECIES Road to DRILL GROUND Corner with all speed and thence to advance on ROUTE DE LANDRECIES.

Battalion (less D. Company) left at 10.30, arriving at DRILL GROUND Corner at 12.15 and picking up D. Company there. Major F.E. [illegible] and [illegible] other ranks were wounded here by Machine Gun fire from a British aeroplane. 2/Lt. L. Briggs-Lawrance took over command of A. Company.

At 12.[illegible] Battalion advanced astride the ROUTE DE LANDRECIES in following order: A. C. B. D. HQ.

At 13.10 Battalion passed through 1[illegible]th Black Watch (at [illegible] G.[illegible]). Touch could not be obtained with units on either flank, and no information was forthcoming as to the location of the enemy. Battalion continued to advance through the FORET DE MORMAL in artillery formation, with the left flank on the [illegible] side of the ROUTE DE LANDRECIES and the right flank along the Railway - C.Coy on left; A.Coy in centre; B.Coy. on right; D.Coy in support. [illegible] in G.6. [illegible] was reached about 14.00.

At this time heavy fighting was heard from about G.1[illegible].d. and as the right flank was entirely exposed, two Platoons of D. Coy. (under Capt. [illegible] Flook) were ordered to proceed to the ridge in G.12.d. and H.7.c., with instructions to hold this ridge and guard the crossing of the CANAL in H.7.b. On arrival at the ridge, it was found that a post had just been established there by the 2nd R. Dublin Fus. Capt. Flook therefore proceeded N.E. along the railway, and established himself at R.25.c.2.0. to cover the crossing of the CANAL there. At 14.15 touch was obtained with the [illegible] K.R.R.C. on the left at A.24.d.7.4. At about the same time orders were received from [illegible] Brigade to push on as far as possible and get in touch with both flanks.

Slight opposition was now encountered from enemy snipers and Machine Guns. At 15.30 orders were received from Brigade to establish line from R.21.d.20.45 (exclusive) to the CANAL with a post on Bridge at R.27.d.

By 16.30 line had been established from spur in R.20.d. to Railway at [illegible] - C.Coy on left, 2 platoons of A.Coy. in centre, B.Coy on right: 2 platoons of A.Coy. and 2 platoons of D.Coy. in support with Battalion H.Q. at R.25.b.5.5. Darkness prevented further advance and line was consolidated. 2/Lt. L. Briggs-Lawrance was evacuated to Hospital on the night of the 4th suffering from Shell-shock and Lieut. T. Rothwell, M.C. assumed command of A.Company.

At 19.45 under orders from Brigade, the 4th K.R.R.C. relieved C.Company on the left who thereupon side-stepped to the right, the Battalion line now running through R.26.b. to the Railway.

At 01.00 on the 5th November orders were received to continue the advance at 06.30. Battalion objective, line of CANAL, from R.29.c.2.9. to R.24.c.5.7. Bridge heads to be established at THE HALT. R.27.d.05.75 and at ECLUSE HACHETTE R.23.d. with preliminary artillery barrage - 2 18 pdr guns also being at the disposal of the Battalion.

[illegible] Patrols were sent out by B. Company during the night and reported that the houses at THE HALT were occupied by the enemy. At 05.00 a platoon of B.Company was pushed forward along the Railway to cover the crossing at THE HALT, and reached a point about R.27.a.7.3.

Advance was continued at 06.30 - C.Coy. on left, B.Coy. on right. A.Coy. and 2 platoons of D.Coy in support. Machine Gun opposition was encountered from the houses at THE HALT. This position was taken by 06.40. Considerable hostile shell fire was encountered, also severe opposition from snipers and strong Machine Gun posts in houses in HACHETTE. These posts were rushed and the guns and their gunners either killed or captured at R.28.b.0.4. and R.25.d.3.2. By 08.30, the line was established along the CANAL from R.29.c.2.9. to [illegible] NOIRE - thence through the Town to about R.23.d.1.7. Posts were also established on the S. Bank of the Canal, at the plank bridge heads in R.22.d. A.Coy. in support N. of the Road in R.23.b. Touch was obtained wi[illegible] R.N.[illegible] on the left. 1 Company of 1st K.O.Y.L.I. [illegible] Battalion to guard the crossing of the CANAL at [illegible] in R.22.D.

[illegible] was taken over b[illegible] Platoons of [illegible] of 1st K.O.Y.L.I. and the 2 Platoons of [illegible] Battalion, B.Coy. being in [illegible] reserve.

[illegible] village of [illegible] and the Railway [illegible] were [illegible] shelled by the enemy during the day, no sign was seen of the enemy on our immediate front, although there [illegible] enemy transport and [illegible] in the direction of NOYELLES. [illegible] during the night of the [illegible] two patrols [illegible] - one to reconnoitre the stream between C.1[illegible].d. and C.1[illegible].b and c. and the other to NOYELLES. Both patrols returned at about 2100 hours without encountering the enemy, although hostile Machine Gun was heard firing from S. of NOYELLES.

On the morning of the 6th November, Battalion left [illegible] at 09.00 and concentrated in Wood in R.2[illegible].c. in very heavy rain. At 1[illegible].0 hours, under orders from Brigade, Battalion moved to [illegible] FARM in R.27.a. where a very hurried meal was prepared. At 1[illegible].30 the Brigade left [illegible] FARM, crossed the CANAL in R.27.c. and marched to Billets at NOYELLES, arriving there at about 1[illegible].00.

Reference map
57A. 1/40,000.

At 0[illegible] on the 7th November, the following orders were received (Ref Operation Order No. 1[illegible]). Brigade to continue the advance, starting out from NOYELLES at 6 a.m. in following order :- 1st K.O.Y.L.I., 6th R. Innis. Fus., 4th [illegible] Route [illegible] - [illegible] - ST. WAAST. Road Junction at D.13.c.5.1. At this point Battalions were to pass through 149th and 150th Brigades and advance to their objective. Battalion 1st objective - ST. AUBIN - AVESNES Road - [illegible] astride Route [illegible] - ST. AUBIN to cross roads [illegible] 5.7. mopping up St. AUBIN. 4th [illegible] on left, 1st K.O.Y.L.I. on right.

Final Objective [illegible] - AVESNES Road from [illegible].d.8.5. to [illegible] 7.7. (exclusive) via road through D.17.d., D.18.c & d., [illegible] & d. No advance to be made beyond 1st objective until orders were received from Brigade.

[illegible] Jumping off point at D.1[illegible].c.5.1. was reached at 0[illegible].15. Advance from here was carried out in following order :- Advance Guard A.Coy. under Lieut. [illegible] (Vanguard under 24281 Sgt. T. [illegible]): Main body - 500 yards distance from Advance Guard - [illegible] astride the route with 100 yards distance between companies. By 09.55 Battalion was completely through the wood in D.14.d. and D.15.c. having met with very slight opposition. Very considerable opposition was encountered from Machine Guns and snipers in the houses in St. AUBIN. The outskirts of this village were reached by the Vanguard at 10.20. While the advanced guard pushed their way through the village, B.Company [illegible] round on the left of the Village and [illegible] Company to the right. [illegible] 11.10 the advanced guard had reached the St. AUBIN - AVESNES Road in [illegible] c. Considerable opposition was encountered from strong Machine Gun posts in sunken road in [illegible] and the two field guns attached to the Battalion were ordered to [illegible] this position, while [illegible] Coy. were also sent forward to work round the flank. By 11.[illegible] the village of St. AUBIN had been completely [illegible] positions on the St. AUBIN - AVESNES Road had been consolidated and posts pushed well forward [illegible] of the road in [illegible]. The enemy was now persistently shelling our positions and also the village of St. AUBIN, while we were also being harassed by snipers and indirect Machine Gun fire [illegible]. At 12.[illegible] Battalion was in touch both with 4th [illegible] on left and 1st K.O.Y.L.I. on right. At 13.30 hours orders were received from Brigade to continue the advance to final objective at 13.50 hours. Advance was accordingly resumed at 10.40. C.Coy acting as Advanced Guard, followed by B, D and A. Companies. 2 Field guns attached to Battalion shelling [illegible] from 12.45 to 14.00.

Considerable opposition was now encountered - both hostile shelling and exceptionally heavy Machine Gun and Rifle fire. Capt. G.L.Henderson was wounded early in the attack and 2/Lt. R.[illegible] Farrell assumed command of C.Coy. At 14.40, C and B. Companies had reached the sunken road in D.18.d. Very strong enemy Machine Gun posts were established in the sunken road in D.18.c. To reach this position a stretch of perfectly open country 400 yards in extent had to be crossed and every attempt was met with very heavy Machine Gun fire, resulting in severe casualties. D.Company was sent up to reinforce and orders were given to B. and C.Companies to endeavour to work round the flanks of the positions. In the face however of the exceptionally strong enemy position, supported by very heavy hostile artillery, Trench Mortar and Machine Gun fire, although repeated attempts to advance were made, they were unsuccessful. Two Field guns shelled the sunken road in D.18.c.from 15.50 to 16.00 but without being able to dislodge the enemy. At 15.50 hours, orders were received from the Brigade that if objective had not been attained by dusk, Battalion was to consolidate in depth. Line was therefore consolidated in sunken road in D.18.d. and along St. AUBIN - MONT DOURLERS Road from D.18.d.7.7. to E.13.c.0.8. B and C. Companies in front line, D. Company in support and A. Company in reserve in the wood in Chateau grounds D.18.c and d.

Advance to final objective was resumed at 07.30 on the 8th November, under artillery barrage, B.Company on the left and A. Company on the right, while D. Company were despatched to work round the right flank and mop up MONT DOURLERS. C.Company remained in support.

In spite of heavy hostile artillery, Machin Gun and Rifle fire, troops advanced with great rapidity and had completely gained their objective by 08.00 hours, and had pushed forward posts well in front of the MAUBEUGE - AVESNES Road. Touch was obtained both with 4th K.R.R.C. on left and 1st K.O.Y.L.I. on right. Considerable opposition was experienced from hostile Machine Gun posts in houses in MONT DOURLERS. These posts were however mopped up by D. Company by 08.30. Enemy artillery at edge of wood in E.22. continued to shell our positions all morning, as also Support Company and Battalion Headquarters in Sunken Road in E.13.c. At about 11.15 enemy attempted a counter-attack from E.21 central, but their infantry were dispersed by our Lewis Gun fire. Under cover of an artillery barrage, however, their Machine Gunners determinedly pushed forward Machine Gun posts from edge of wood in E.22 and also from direction of FLOURSIES. For a time the situation was very critical, but the Artillery rendered valuable assistance by a barrage directed on E.21.central. Our Machine Gunners also rapidly took up commanding positions and their indirect fire on E.21.central was very effective.

Lieut-Colonel G.G.F.F.Greville (in the right arm) and Capt. & Adjt. H.O.Belton (in the head) were both wounded by the same shell at about 12.00, but neither wound was very serious and these officers were able to remain at duty. Counter-attack had died down completely by about 13.00. At 15.30 the [illegible] Infantry Brigade (3rd Royal Fusrs) passed through our line to continue the advance, and at 16.00, the Battalion marched back to billets to St. REMY CHAUSSEE.

Too great testimony cannot be paid to the valuable work rendered by all N.C.Os during these operations. There was a very great shortage of officers and N.C.Os throughout, the shortage gradually increasing with casualties. By the afternoon of the 7th, there were only four officers left with their Companies, Lieut. Rothwell (A): Capt. Lyndon (B): 2/Lt. Turrell (C): and Capt. Flook (D), together with Commanding Officer and Adjutant at Headquarters. The few remaining N.C.O's with the utmost gallantry and skill led their men with the most marked success. In innumerable cases they were entirely dependent on their own initiative and the operations could not have been successful had they not responded so well to the heavy responsibilities laid upon them.

In one particular instance, No. 11656 Sgt E. Cunningham was wounded early in the fighting of the 7th one of the fingers of his right hand being shattered by a bullet. Although suffering the most intense pain, this N.C.O. remained in command of his platoon and was only evacuated to Hospital on the 9th inst. when the Battalion had returned to billets.

The endurance of the troops was also beyond all praise. When the advance was resumed on the morning of the 7th, the men were completely exhausted by seven days continual duty in the front line, by long marching and heavy fighting, and continual exposure to cold and wet since, the 31st October. Despite this, they responded with the utmost cheerfulness to the call made to them. In addition to the heavy fighting that day, they actually marched nearly 10 miles in thick mud, and although under heavy artillery and Machine Gun fire continuously from 11.00 hours on the 7th and suffering heavy casualties, they advanced to their final objective, the following morning with the greatest dash and determination and captured the position with a rapidity which would have been remarkable even with completely fresh troops.

<u>Casualties from 31st October to 8th November</u>.

<u>Officers</u>.:-

Wounded and Missing.	1.
Wounded at duty.	2.
Wounded.	5.
Total.	8.

<u>Other Ranks</u>.

Killed.	30.
Wounded and Missing.	2
Missing.	2.
Wounded.	154.

<u>Captures, 31st October to 8th November</u>.

3 Officers and approximately 80 Other ranks.
1 5.9 Gun: 1 Field gun (about 18 pdr). and
approximately 15 to 20 Machine Guns.

Vol 12

Confidential

War Diary

6th ROYAL INNISKILLING FUSILIERS

1st To 31st December 1918

Volume XLII

Instructions regarding War Diaries and Intelligence Summaries are contained in F. S. Regs., Part II. and the Staff Manual respectively. Title pages will be prepared in manuscript.

WAR DIARY
or
INTELLIGENCE SUMMARY.
(Erase heading not required.)

Army Form C. 2118.

Place	Date	Hour	Summary of Events and Information	Remarks and references to Appendices

D. D. & L., London, E.C.
(A8004) Wt. W1771/M2-31 750,000 5/17 **Sch. 52** Forms/C2118/14

Army Form C. 2118.

Instructions regarding War Diaries and Intelligence Summaries are contained in F. S. Regs., Part II. and the Staff Manual respectively. Title pages will be prepared in manuscript.

WAR DIARY
or
~~INTELLIGENCE SUMMARY.~~
(Erase heading not required.)

6th Royal Inniskilling Fus.
Volume XLII
December 1918 - page 1.

Place	Date	Hour	Summary of Events and Information	Remarks and references to Appendices
MONCEAU	1918 1st Dec.		Sunday. Usual Church parades. Battalion Gymkhana held this afternoon	HOB
	2nd		Battalion Route march in full marching order - LEVAL, NOYELLES and TAISNIERES. Lecture on "Astronomy" at 1400 in Brigade Reading Room. Football match - Officers 6 goals: W.O's + N.C.O's 2. Educational Classes (French, Reading + Writing, Bookkeeping) 17.30 to 19.30	HOB
	3rd		Division visited by H. M. The King this morning. Battalion paraded on both sides of ST REMY - AVESNES Road (about D. 2. A. 5. 7 - Sheet 57A - 1/40,000) at 11.00. H. M. The King arrived at 11.35 hours, and walked along the road, inspecting each Battalion in turn	HOB
	4th		Advance parties sent on to new billets at OBIES. No parades or class. 21 other ranks joined from HAUDRICOURT today (from party left at MARTIN EGLISE on 16th Sept.)	HOB
	5th	0930	Battalion left MONCEAU at 0930 and marched via AULNOYE Sta., PONT-SUR-SAMBRE and MACQUIGNIES to OBIES, arriving	
OBIES		1400	there at 1400. Marching-out State (including advance party) A 82: B 77: C 96: D 82: HQ 135 = Total 472 Officers 31	HOB
	6th		Battalion cleaning-up village, improving billets &c. Brigadier + Divisional Commanders both visited billets today	HOB
	7th		Training: 1 hours arms drill. Rest of morning spent in cleaning-up. Usual Educational classes resumed this afternoon	HOB
	8th		Sunday. Usual C. of E. parade. R.C's attended Voluntary Mass in Village Church. Football - Rest of Battalion 2: H.Q. coy 1. Transport lines and billets inspected by both Brigadier + Divisional Commander today	HOB

D. D. & L., London, E.C. (A8004) Wt. W1771/M2 31 750,000 5/17 Sch. 52 Forms/C2118/14

Instructions regarding War Diaries and Intelligence Summaries are contained in F. S. Regs., Part II. and the Staff Manual respectively. Title pages will be prepared in manuscript.

WAR DIARY
or
~~INTELLIGENCE SUMMARY.~~
(Erase heading not required.)

Army Form C. 2118.

6th Royal Inniskilling Fus.
Volume XLII
December 1918 - page 2.

Place	Date	Hour	Summary of Events and Information	Remarks and references to Appendices
OBIES	1918 Dec. 9th		Training - Arms Drill - Lewis Gun. Educational class in the morning (10.30 to 12.30). Company league football - D. Coy 5 : B. Coy. 2	KOB
	10th		Training and classes as usual.	KOB
	11th		do. Football - D. Coy 3 : C. Coy. 2	KOB
	12th		do.	KOB
	13th		do. First Demobilizer left for U.K. today.	KOB
	14th		do. 18 miners left for U.K. today making 26 despatched to date	KOB
	15th		Sunday. Usual C. of E. parade. No service for R. Cs except in Village Church	KOB
	16th		Usual training - Musketry on 30x Range. Lewis Gun training. Educational classes	KOB
	17th		Training and classes as usual.	KOB
	18th		do.	
	19th		Wet today. Lewis gun training in Billets. C.O's lecture to Subaltern officers on Kings regulations. Classes as usual. Divisional inter Company football Competition. HQ Coy. R. Innis Fus 9 goals. KOYLI 3 goals. 16 Other Ranks joined from hospital. Medical Officer left today.	KOB HLG

D. D. & L., London, E.C.
(A8004) Wt. W1771/M2-31 750,000 5/17 Sch. 52 Forms/C2118/14

Instructions regarding War Diaries and Intelligence Summaries are contained in F. S. Regs., Part II. and the Staff Manual respectively. Title pages will be prepared in manuscript.

WAR DIARY
or
~~INTELLIGENCE SUMMARY.~~
(Erase heading not required.)

6th Royal Inniskilling Fusiliers Army Form C. 2118.
Volume XLII.
December 1918 page 3.

Place	Date	Hour	Summary of Events and Information	Remarks and references to Appendices
OBIES	1918 20th Dec		Wet again to day Route March Cancelled - Lewis Gun training in Billets Educational Classes as usual. C.O's lecture to Subaltern Officers on Kings Regulations	JRLG
	21st Dec		Route March this morning. Classes in the afternoon as usual	JRLG
	22nd		C of E Service in Schoolroom at 09.00 hours (Voluntary) no classes Band played in the Square in the afternoon	JRLG
	23rd		Rehearsal for Lewis Gun Competition. Football Match against Div Signals No Score. Classes as usual	JRLG
	24th		Cross Country run and Lewis Gun Competion in Morning. 37 miners left for U.K.	JRLG
	25th		C of E Service Voluntary at 09.30 hours. Football Match. H.Q. Coy v. Rest of Battn. 'The Rest' won 2-0 goals. Race Meeting in afternoon Evening Concert & dance. Christmas trees given by the men for the French children Lewis Gun team went to Bde H.Q. for prizes.	JRLG

D. D. & L., London, E.C. (A8004) Wt. W1771/M2 31 750,000 5/17 Sch. 52 Forms/C2118/14.

Instructions regarding War Diaries and Intelligence Summaries are contained in F. S. Regs., Part II. and the Staff Manual respectively. Title pages will be prepared in manuscript.

WAR DIARY or ~~INTELLIGENCE SUMMARY.~~

(Erase heading not required.)

Army Form C. 2118.

6th Royal Inniskilling Fusiliers
Volume XLII
December 1918 Page 4

Place	Date	Hour	Summary of Events and Information	Remarks and references to Appendices
OBIES	1918 Dec 26	Dec	Interior Economy - No parades - No Classes.	[initials]
	27th		Reconnaissance for Salvage by Officers. C.O's parade. Classes as usual	[initials]
	28th		Too wet for Salvage - Interior Economy - and Classes.	[initials]
	29th		C of E Service in Schoolroom	[initials]
	30th		Salvage carried out by Companies. Classes as usual.	
	31st		Salvage carried out by Companies - Classes as usual. Played Semifinal Divisional Company league against Divisional Signals Result. Inniskillings won. Score 1 - 0.	[initials]

[signature] Major
Cmdg 6. R. Innis. Fus.

D. D. & L., London, E.C. (A8004) Wt. W1771/M2'31 750,000 5/17 Sch. 52 Forms/C2118/14

WAR DIARY

6TH BN ROYAL INNISKILLING FUSILIERS

JANUARY 1919

VOL XLIII

Instructions regarding War Diaries and Intelligence Summaries are contained in F. S. Regs., Part II. and the Staff Manual respectively. Title pages will be prepared in manuscript.

WAR DIARY
or
INTELLIGENCE SUMMARY.
(Erase heading not required.)

Army Form C. 2118.

6th Royal Inniskilling Fusiliers
Volume XLIII
page 1 January 1919

Place	Date	Hour	Summary of Events and Information	Remarks and references to Appendices
OBIES	1919. 1st Jan.		Battalion engaged on salvage work. No classes of instruction. Ration strength 33 officers - 435 other ranks	HOB
	2nd		Battalion paraded to say "good-bye" to Brig-Gen. R. E. Sugden. No salvage work. Classes of instruction in the afternoon.	HOB
	3rd		Salvage work and classes of instruction (Reading and Writing, Bookkeeping, French, Shorthand) as usual	HOB
	4th		Salvage work + classes as usual	HOB
	5th		Sunday. C. of E. Voluntary service at 0930. Final of Divisional inter-company football competition:- 2/2nd Northumbrian Field Ambulance 5 goals: HQ Coy. 6th R Innis Fus. - Nil	HOB
			3 men left today for demobilization	
	6th		Salvage work and classes as usual. Average attendance at present Reading + Writing 32 : Shorthand 10 : Bookkeeping 16 : French 14	HOB
			3 men left today for demobilization.	
	7th		Salvage work and classes as usual. Also 1 hours arms drill	HOB
	8th		Battalion bathing, washing clothes and general work of interior economy	HOB
	9th		Salvage and classes as usual. One Company working on roads. G.O.C. 50th Div. inspected billets &c. this morning	HOB
	10th		Salvage, Road work and classes as yesterday	HOB
	11th		do also 2 hours training.	
			Salvage work now completed except for the transfer of the dumps of ammunition &c. to central dumps at BAVAI and LE QUESNOY Divisional inter-battalion football: Scottish Horse 8 goals: 6th R. Innis. Fus. 2 goals	HOB
	12th		Sunday Voluntary C. of E. service 0930 hours Divisional Cinema at OBIES today	HOB

D. D. & L., London, E.C. (A8004) Wt. W1771/M2-31 750,000 5/17 Sch. 52 Forms/C2118/14

Army Form C. 2118.

Instructions regarding War Diaries and Intelligence Summaries are contained in F. S. Regs., Part II. and the Staff Manual respectively. Title pages will be prepared in manuscript.

WAR DIARY
or
INTELLIGENCE SUMMARY.
(Erase heading not required.)

6th Royal Inniskilling Fus
Volume XLIII
page 2 January 1919.

Place	Date	Hour	Summary of Events and Information	Remarks and references to Appendices
OBIES.	1919 13th Jan.		Salvage, Road work, training and classes as usual. 3 men left for demobilization	HOB
	14th		do Divisional Cinema at OBIES for past three days. 7 men left today for demobilization	HOB
	15th		All companies marched to BAVAI for hot baths. No classes or salvage work.	HOB
	16th		Battalion training; one company on salvage; usual classes	HOB
	17th		do. usual classes; no salvage work	HOB
			2/Lt. W. J. Fulton and 21 men left today for demobilization	HOB
	18th		Training, Salvage and Classes as usual	
	19th		Sunday Voluntary C. of E. service 0900 hours	HOB
			1 man left today for demobilization	HOB
	20th		Training, Salvage and Classes today as usual	
			Lecture on "Demobilization" by Capt. F. E. Moore	
			3 men left today for demobilization	
	21st		Training, Salvage and Classes as usual. 26 men left today for demobilization	HOB
	22nd		Combined rehearsal (5th R. Irish Regmt, 7th Bn Wiltshire Regmt & this Battn) of Ceremony for consecration of colours.	HOB
			No classes or salvage work	
	23rd		Training, Classes and Salvage as usual. Lieut-Col. G. G. F. F. Greville, D.S.O. rejoined today and re-assumed command of Battalion	HOB
	24th		Battalion Route March. 35 men left today for U.K. for demobilization	HOB

D. D. & L., London, E.C. (A8004) Wt. W1771/M2031 750,000 5/17 Sch. 52 Forms/C2118/14

Army Form C. 2118.

Instructions regarding War Diaries and Intelligence Summaries are contained in F. S. Regs., Part II. and the Staff Manual respectively. Title pages will be prepared in manuscript.

WAR DIARY
or
INTELLIGENCE SUMMARY.
(Erase heading not required.)

6th Royal Inniskilling Fus

Volume XLIII

page 3 — January 1919.

Place	Date	Hour	Summary of Events and Information	Remarks and references to Appendices
OBIES.	25th		Training and classes as usual. Shorthand class discontinued 9 men left today for demobilization	HCB
	26th		Sunday. No Church services owing to snowstorm.	HCB
	27th		Battalion Route march – Classes as usual. Weather too severe for salvage 2/Lt. H. A. Whiteside & 22 men left today for demobilization	HCB
	28th		Battalion training and clearing snow from roads. Classes as usual	HCB
	29th		All companies firing on 100 yards range. No classes	HCB
	30th		Training, salvage and classes as usual	HCB
	31st		do. do. Average attendance of classes at present – Reading and Writing 28; French 8; Bookkeeping 8. 7 men left today for demobilization. Ration strength 31 officers 295 other ranks	HCB

G. J. Greville Lieut.-Col.,
Commanding 6th R. INNISKILLING FUS.

1/2/19

D. D. & L., London, E.C.
(A8004) Wt. W1771/M2731 750,000 5/17 Sch. 52 Forms/C2118/14

Confidential

War Diary

6th Royal Inniskilling Fusiliers

1st to 28th February 1919

Volume XLIV

Instructions regarding War Diaries and Intelligence Summaries are contained in F. S. Regs., Part II. and the Staff Manual respectively. Title pages will be prepared in manuscript.

WAR DIARY
or
~~INTELLIGENCE SUMMARY.~~
(Erase heading not required.)

Army Form C. 2118.

6th Royal Inniskilling Fus.
Volume XLIV
February 1919 - Page 1

Place	Date	Hour	Summary of Events and Information	Remarks and references to Appendices
OBIES.	1919 1st		Battalion Route march 8 men to U.K. for demobilization. Lecture by Adjutant on terms &c. of new Army of Occupation. Ration strength 29 officers - 287 other ranks. Total number of men re-enlisting, up to date, 40	HOB
	2nd		Voluntary C of E and Presbyterian services. Lieut. J. Rothwell, M.C. and 30 men left for U.K. for demobilization	HOB
	3rd		Training 0900 to 11.30. Commanding Officer, 6 officers + 14 men went by lorry to visit LE CATEAU battlefield	HOB
	4th		Training - all morning	HOB
	5th		do. 2/Lt. G. Porter and 11 men left for U.K. for demobilization.	HOB
	6th		Training - all morning	HOB
	7th		do. 24 men to U.K. for demobilization. 6 officers and 36 other ranks went to WATERLOO and BRUSSELLS today, in 2 lorries; returning tomorrow	HOB
	8th		Training as usual	HOB
	9th		Sunday. Presbyterian service only	HOB
	10th		Training as usual. Lewis Gun + Musketry classes for Army of Occupation draft	HOB
	11th		ditto.	HOB
	12th		ditto. 4 men to U.K. for demobilization	HOB

D. D. & L., London, E.C. (A8004) Wt. W1771/M2531 750,000 5/17 Sch. 52 Forms/C2118/14

Instructions regarding War Diaries and Intelligence Summaries are contained in F. S. Regs., Part II. and the Staff Manual respectively. Title pages will be prepared in manuscript.

WAR DIARY
or
~~INTELLIGENCE SUMMARY.~~
(*Erase heading not required.*)

Army Form C. 2118.

6th Royal Inniskilling Fus.
Volume XLIV
February 1919 - page 2

Place	Date	Hour	Summary of Events and Information	Remarks and references to Appendices
OBIES	13th		Training and classes for Army of Occupation draft as usual. 16 men to U.K. for demobilization. Thaw now set in after over 3 weeks hard frost.	HOB
	14th		Draft inspected by G.O.C. 50th Division (57 on parade)	HOB
	15th		23 men to U.K. for demobilization. Ration strength - 25 officers - 189 other ranks	HOB
	16th		Sunday. R.C., C. of E. and Presbyterian services	HOB
	17th		Training as usual	HOB
	18th		do.	HOB
	19th		do. 14 men to U.K. for demobilization	HOB
	20th		do 2 do.	HOB
	21st		27 men to U.K. for demobilization	HOB
	22nd	0930	Battalion left OBIES at 0930 and marched to billets at ENGLEFONTAINE, arriving at 13.30. Marching-out state - 22 officers - 147 other ranks. 3 men to U.K. for demobilization	HOB
ENGLEFONTAINE	23rd		Sunday. Cleaning up billets all day - no services	HOB
	24th		Cleaning and improving billets	HOB
	25th		3 officers + 289 other ranks attached from 5th R. Irish Regiment (Pioneers) and billeted in HECQ	HOB
	26th		1 man to U.K. for demobilization - also 40 from 5th R. Irish Regt	HOB
	27th		13 do. 38 do	HOB
	28th		4 do.	

G. J. Greville Lieut.-Col.,
Commanding 6th R. INNISKILLING FUS.

D. D. & L., London, E.C. (A8004) Wt. W1771/M2 31 750,000 5/17 Sch. 52 Forms/C2118/14

D.8. 36 J

WL 15

Confidential

War Diary

6th Royal Inniskilling Fusiliers

1st to 31st March 1919.

Volume XLV

Army Form C. 2118.

WAR DIARY

~~or~~

~~INTELLIGENCE SUMMARY.~~

(Erase heading not required.)

Instructions regarding War Diaries and Intelligence Summaries are contained in F. S. Regs., Part II. and the Staff Manual respectively. Title pages will be prepared in manuscript.

6th Royal Inniskilling Fus
Volume XLV
March 1919 - page 1

Place	Date	Hour	Summary of Events and Information	Remarks and references to Appendices
ENGLEFONTAINE	1st		5 officers (Capt C.N. Flook and 2/Lts J. Ellison, B.E. Nicholls, J.E. Phillips + W.B. Phipps) left today to join 7/8th Royal Inniskilling Fus, 30th Division at BOULOGNE (Army of Occupation)	
			2 men to U.K. for demobilization, also 1 man from R. Irish Regmt	HOB
			Battalion Ration strength - 16 officers 87 ors: Irish Regmt 3 officers 194 ors.	
	2nd		Sunday. Summer time adopted at midnight 1st/2nd	HOB
	3rd		Ration strength - 16 officers 86 ors: Irish Regmt 3 officers 190 ors.	HOB
	4th		8 "Z" mules sent to LE QUESNOY for sale today.	HOB
	5th		21 men of R. Irish Regmt. to U.K. for demobilization	HOB
			Ration strength - 14 officers 93 ors: Irish Regmt 3 officers 161 ors	
	6th		6 men to U.K. for demobilization + 79 from Irish Regmt	HOB
	7th		41 men of R. Irish Regmt for demobilization today + 1 officer	HOB
	8th		9 men to U.K. for demobilization	HOB
			Ration strength - 9 officers 77 ors: Irish Regmt 2 officers 32 ors.	
			Remainder of Irish Regmt. details moved in from HECQ to ENGLEFONTAINE	
	9th		9 men to U.K. for demobilization + 1 officer and 1 man from Irish Regmt	HOB
	10th		Rehearsal for Colour ceremony - at LOWENDAL Barrack Square, LE QUESNOY	HOB
	11th		Battalion rehearsal for Colour ceremony	HOB
	12th		9 men to U.K. for demobilization and 26 from Irish Regmt	HOB
	13th		Ration strength - 9 officers 62 ors: Irish Regmt 1 officer 24 ors.	HOB
	14th		Field Marshal Commander-in-Chief at Div H.Q. LE QUESNOY to see Div. Bde and Battn commanders	HOB
	15th		Lieut S.A. Drysdale + 2/Lt W. Armstrong left today for demobilization. 3 escaped German prisoners captured in the forest	HOB

D. D. & L., London, E.C.
(A5004) Wt. W1771/M2-31 750,000 5/17 Sch. 52 Forms/C2118/14

Instructions regarding War Diaries and Intelligence Summaries are contained in F. S. Regs., Part II. and the Staff Manual respectively. Title pages will be prepared in manuscript.

WAR DIARY

~~or~~

~~INTELLIGENCE SUMMARY.~~

(Erase heading not required.)

Army Form C. 2118.

6th Royal Inniskilling Fusiliers
Volume XLV
March 1919. page 2

Place	Date	Hour	Summary of Events and Information	Remarks and references to Appendices
ENGLEFONTAINE	16th		3 men for demobilization today + 18 from R. Irish Regiment	HJB
	17th		Ration strength 10 officers 67 ors: Irish Regmt. 2 officers 8 ors.	HJB
	18th		8 Riding horses sent away today - 2 others retained, unfit to travel	HJB
	19th		4 men to U.K. for demobilization	HJB
	20th		Ration strength 10 officers 59 ors: Irish Regmt. 4 officers 9 ors.	HJB
	21st		do 11 " 62 " do 4 " 9 "	HJB
	22nd		All leave and demobilization temporarily suspended, owing to threatened general Railway strike at home	HJB
	23rd		Ration strength 10 officers 63 ors: Irish Regmt 4 officers 9 ors.	HJB
	24th		2/Lt A. J. Racey + 4 officers of R. Irish Regmt (Capt E. Errington, Capt W. B. Baillie, Lieuts E. Healy + V. Hunter) also 10 men from Battn. + 4 from R. Irish Regmt. left for demobilization today. (All 1914 and 1915 officers can now be demobilized) Remaining 2 riding horses sent away today.	HJB
	25th		Ration strength: 8 officers 52 ors: Irish Regmt. 5 ors.	HJB
	26th		do 9 " 53 " do 1 officer, 5 ors.	HJB
	27th		Advance party sent to new billets at POTELLE	HJB
	28th		Battalion left ENGLEFONTAINE at 10.30 and marched to	
POTELLE			POTELLE, arriving at 12.00	HJB
	29th		Very cold - snowing all day. 13 mules to M.V.S. today	HJB
	30th		4 men for demobilization, also Lieut H. L. Roche + 3 men of Irish Regmt	HJB
	31st		4 men on leave today. Ration strength 11 officers 44 ors: also 10 ors of R. Irish Regmt. Away on leave, extra-regimental employment etc. 11 officers 26 ors: R. Irish Regmt. 3 officers 17 ors:	

G. F. Greville Lieut.-Col.,
Commanding 6th R. Innis. Fus.

D. D. & L., London, E.C. (A8004) Wt. W1771/M2731 750,000 5/17 Sch. 52 Forms/C2118/14

Confidential

War Diary

6th ROYAL INNISKILLING FUSILIERS

1st to 30th April 1919

Volume XLVI

Instructions regarding War Diaries and Intelligence Summaries are contained in F. S. Regs., Part II. and the Staff Manual respectively. Title pages will be prepared in manuscript.

WAR DIARY
~~or~~
~~INTELLIGENCE SUMMARY.~~
(Erase heading not required.)

Army Form C. 2118.

6th Royal Inniskilling Fus.
Volume XLVI
April 1919 - page 1.

Place	Date	Hour	Summary of Events and Information	Remarks and references to Appendices
POTELLE	1st		Ration strength - 10 officers - 45 ors - also 10 ors. R. Irish Regmt.	HOB
	2nd		3 other ranks left today for 7/8th Battn (Army of Occupation)	HOB
	3rd		151st Bde H.Q. removed to POTELLE chateau	HOB
	4th		Last 6 mules sent away for demobilization today - 5 horses sent to Battalion to replace	HOB
	5th		Ration strength - 9 officers - 41 other ranks: Irish Regmt. 2 officers 11 ors. Total 11 officers - 52 other ranks	HOB
	6th		2/Lt. H. J. Beazer left for demobilization today - also 2 officers + 6 men of R. Irish Regmt.	HOB
	7th		2/Lts. E. H. G. THORNE, A. P. PARKER and A. J. WELLS left today for duty with D.A.D.G.R.+E., Third Army	HOB
	8th		Ration strength 9 officers - 41 other ranks, also 5 ors. R. Irish Regmt	HOB
	9th		Football match - Battn. 3 goals: 4th K.R.R.C. Nil	HOB
	10th		Ration strength - 9 officers - 41 other ranks (also 5 ors R. Irish Regmt) Effective strength 17 officers - 66 other ranks.	HOB
	11th		Ration strength 9 officers - 40 other ranks (also 5 ors. R. Irish Regmt)	HOB
	12th		do.	HOB
	13th		2/Lt G. Johnston + 2 other ranks left for demobilization Football - 2nd + 4th K.R.R.C. 4 goals - Battn + Bde HQ. 1 goal	HOB
	14th		Ration strength 10 officers - 37 other ranks (also 5 ors. R. Irish Regmt)	HOB
	15th		do 10 do 38 do 5 do	HOB

D. D. & L., London, E.C. (A8004) Wt. W1771/M2 31 750,000 5/17 Sch. 52 Forms/C2118/14

Instructions regarding War Diaries and Intelligence Summaries are contained in F. S. Regs., Part II. and the Staff Manual respectively. Title pages will be prepared in manuscript.

WAR DIARY ~~or INTELLIGENCE SUMMARY.~~

(Erase heading not required.)

6th Royal Inniskilling Fus
Volume XLVI
April 1919 - page 2

Army Form C. 2118.

Place	Date	Hour	Summary of Events and Information	Remarks and references to Appendices
POTELLE	16th		C.O. + Adj. went to PROSPECT HILL today, to erect crosses over graves	HSB
	17th		Ration strength 10 officers 38 other ranks (also 5 ors. R. Irish Regmt). Effective strength - 13 officers 59 other ranks)	HSB
	18th		Good Friday. 4 men of Irish Regmt. left today for 7th R Irish Regmt	HSB
	19th		Last man of R. Irish Regmt. (Pte Kelly) sent to Prison today. Quarter guard now abolished. Draft of 4 men arrived. Started cricket practice today.	HSB
	20th		Easter Day. 3 horses sent away - only 2 now left	HSB
	21st		Ration strength - 10 officers - 37 other ranks.	HSB
	22nd		Capt J. D. Martin + 2/Lts W. A. B. Dunn, C. R. Booth + H Phillips left today to join P. of W. Coys 2 men of R. Irish Regmt. rejoined.	HSB
	23rd		2/Lt. H. Holden left today for duty with DADGR+E, No 3 Area	HSB
	24th		Owner of Chateau arrived + took over half the building. Ration strength 5 officers - 44 other ranks. Effective do. 6 do. 54 do	HSB
	25th		Major Lyndon + Bde Major went to PROSPECT HILL to erect crosses over graves	HSB
	26th		Inter-Battn. Football - 1st round - 2nd K.R.R.C. 3: Battn. Nil	
			Major G. C. B. Lyndon left today - to command 74 P. of W. Coy	HSB
	27th		5 men left for demobilization - also 2 of R. Irish Regmt	HSB
	28th		Lt. Col. Greville left today for leave in the U.K.	HSB
	29th		Ration strength - 3 officers - 34 other ranks	HSB
	30th		2 men left today for 7/8th Bn. R. Innis. Fus	HSB

30/4/19

H Bolton Capt
Commanding 6th R. INNISKILLING FUS.

D. D. & L., London, E.C. (A8004) Wt. W1771/M2731 750,000 5/17 Sch. 52 Forms/C2118/14

Confidential

War Diary

6th ROYAL INNISKILLING FUSILIERS

1st to 31st May 1919

Volume XLVII

Instructions regarding War Diaries and Intelligence Summaries are contained in F. S. Regs., Part II. and the Staff Manual respectively. Title pages will be prepared in manuscript.

WAR DIARY
~~or~~
~~INTELLIGENCE SUMMARY.~~
(Erase heading not required.)

6th Royal Inniskilling Fus
Volume XLVII
May 1919 - page 1.

Army Form C. 2118.

Place	Date	Hour	Summary of Events and Information	Remarks and references to Appendices
TOTELLE	1st		Ration strength of Battalion 3 officers 33 other ranks Effective do 5 do 49 do	HOB
	2nd		Orders received today that Cadre is to be reduced to 3 officers + 36 men.	HOB
	7th		Divisional Heats for Corps Sports today. No entries from this Cadre.	HOB
	10th		XIII Corps Sports at CAUDRY. No competitors from this Cadre. Motor lorry provided to take 2 officer + 12 men to see the Sports	HOB
	12th		2 Cpls + 5 men left today for demobilization	HOB
	14th		Corps Packet Commander inspected billets today 2 men left today for demobilization	HOB
	17th		1 man do	HOB
	20th		2/Lt J. E. C. Glasson left today upon re-posting to P. of W. Coy	HOB
	21st		Lieut-Col. G. J. F. F. Greville rejoined today from leave	HOB
	24th		1 Cpl. left today on reposting to 7/8th R. Innis. Fus	HOB
	27th		XIII Corps Picnic today at HACHETTE.	
	31st		Ration strength of Cadre 3 officers 31 other ranks Effective strength 4 do 39 do During the month, all available men have been employed in the mornings in clearing up the grounds of Totelle Chateau. Cricket pitch + net provided for recreation in the afternoon. Canteen has been kept well supplied - Beer obtained (under Cadre arrangements) from DOUR (Belgium) and Cigarettes from England. Rations have been supplemented by free issues out of Canteen profits	HOB

G. J. Greville Lieut.-Col.,
Commanding 6th R. INNISKILLING FUS.

31/5/19

D. D. & L., London, E.C.
(A10266) Wt W5300/P713 750,000 2/18 Sch. 52 Forms/C2118/16.

www.ingramcontent.com/pod-product-compliance
Lightning Source LLC
Chambersburg PA
CBHW081448160426
43193CB00013B/2413